The Economy and Meaningfulness. A Utopia?

PETER LANG
Bruxelles • Bern • Berlin • New York • Oxford • Wien

Philosophy & Politics

Volume 30

Series directed by
Hendrik Opdebeeck

Open to thinkers from all countries and cultures who are not limiting their efforts to understand the processes of social institutions, but are raising questions about their goals and meaning, this series hopes to contribute to a renewal of political philosophy. Beyond the different disciplines of social sciences, ideological commitments and the limits of "national schools" philosophy is bound to pursue its universal enquiry on human wisdom in a world chaotically pushed towards greater unity.

Hendrik Opdebeeck

The Economy and Meaningfulness. A Utopia?

Bibliographic information published by "Die Deutsche Nationalbibliothek".
"Die Deutsche National Bibliothek" lists this publication in the "Deutsche Nationalbibliografie"; detailed bibliographic data is available on the Internet at <http://dnb.de>.

This book is the English edition of *Zingeving in economie. Een utopie?* (Kalmthout/Antwerp, Pelckmans Pro, 2016 –ISBN 978-94-6337-023-3).

ISSN 1376-0920 • ISBN 978-2-8076-0964-8 (Print)
E-ISBN 978-2-8076-0965-5 (ePDF) • E-ISBN 978-2-8076-0966-2 (EPUB)
E-ISBN 978-2-8076-0967-9 (MOBI) • DOI 10.3726/b15232
D/2018/5678/108

This publication has been peer reviewed.

International Academic Publishers
Brussels, 2018
1 avenue Maurice, B-1050 Bruxelles, Belgium

www.peterlang.com

Table of Contents

Foreword by Herman Van Rompuy

Our societies and economies have never been as shaken as they have been in recent decades by globalization, digitization and vast migration flows, by the commercialization of every human activity – even the most intimate and exalted. The concepts of financial and monetary stability stand in diametric opposition to the rampant changeability and instability of working life. The multiple crises of the past decade have made people feel like pawns of financial powers, of large multinational companies and of uncontrolled migration movements, and have further heightened feelings of alienation and impotence. People need stability, anchors and certainties. 'Disruption' has become a buzzword. For many people, this has resulted in a great deal of confusion and anxiety. The simple question that is often posed is, 'Where are we heading?'. Underlying this simple question is another age-old question, drawn from a once-famous Flemish book: *Moeder, waarom leven wij?* (*Mother, Why Are We Alive?*). The directions taken in society and in our personal lives are closely connected to each other. Both involve a search. But technology is not the only force up-ending all of our values and certainties. Climate change and the potential exhaustion of natural resources and raw materials have raised questions of meaningfulness. In times of confusion, we must once again go in search of the essence – the meaningfulness behind everything that we do. Have we forgotten that the ultimate aim of an economy and a societal framework is to benefit individual people? Nothing but this should be an end unto itself. For Professor Opdebeeck, everything revolves around personalism. How many people do we bring into fruition through everything that we do? There is a Mozart in all of us but we must not murder him, as Saint-Exupéry once said. Sustainability is more than simply a matter of justice here and elsewhere in the world, or of ecological awareness. Without love for people, there can be no sufficient motivation to turn the tide, and nothing sustainable can emerge. People will resist injustice and self-destruction. Sometimes, they will even seek solace in false prophets, as well as in dangerous ideas and those who herald them. These are the extremes to which despair can bring us. We must therefore provide a response to the greatest deficit of all: the ethical and affective deficit. We must restore the true humanism to which personalism is such a strong testimony. It must permeate our economy. In addition to social and ecological corrections, the market economy is in need of a human correction. Only then will we be able to restore hope and faith in society. European societies are being consumed by negative feelings and anxiety. This is also why they have become so volatile. Only love in all of its forms can provide an injection of hope. There is a need for new leadership, too, which can embody these values. Authenticity could bring back credibility and trust. Professor Opdebeeck clearly demonstrates that meaningfulness is indispensable to the economy.

Herman Van Rompuy

Former President of the European Council

Preface

In 1985, the Jesuit rector of the University of Antwerp, Louis Van Bladel, appointed me to supervise a research project to explore the cultural and philosophical aspects of the economic crisis. From then on, I have been teaching philosophy and ethics to future philosophers, economists, sociologists, business engineers, communications experts, film professionals, politicians and, last but not least, specialists in environmental science. Time and again, the economic and social activities I observe remind me of the topicality of the personalist philosophy of thinkers such as Paul Ricœur and Emanuel Levinas. This philosophy has shaped the basis of my research and teaching. Rephrasing Joseph Amato (2002), to me, a personalist is anyone who, out of respect for the human person, aspires to defend man against individualism as well as collectivism. As I am regularly asked about my personalist foundations, both as chairman of the pluralistic SPES (Spirituality in Economics and Society) think tank, which explores meaningfulness in the economy and society, and by my students and colleagues, I felt compelled to explore the core of this philosophy, related to the economy, in a relatively accessible book.

While I was inspired by a great number of past and present philosophers and economists, I do not intend this book to be an encyclopaedic guide to economic philosophy. On the other hand, I wanted to mark the 500th anniversary of the publication of Thomas More's *Utopia*. For me, this was a dream opportunity to test my personalist background against the well-known vision on utopia and economy of the Dutch philosopher Hans Achterhuis. So Hans Achterhuis is the first person I would like to thank on the occasion of the publication of this book. I also want to thank Bob Goudzwaard of the Free University of Amsterdam, who was the supervisor of my PhD and who continued to stimulate me to develop my research on economy and meaningfulness. Thanks also to my first colleagues at the university of Antwerp such as Koen Boey, Wim Thijs, Louis van

Bladel, Antoon Vandevelde, Jef Van Gerwen and Philippe Verbeeck, who constantly encouraged me to combine my economic insights with philosophy. I would also like to thank Luk Bouckaert and Laszlo Zsolnai, who invited me to include my personalist approach when we founded the SPES think tank that developed into the European SPES Institute. Warm words of thanks to Herman Van Rompuy, former President of the European Council, who wrote the Foreword to this book. I also, especially, thank Ludo Abicht who wrote the insightful Afterword, and his son Bart who translated this book from the Dutch original. And last but not least, I thank my dear partner Johanna-Maria, my children, parents, relatives and friends, and my current colleagues of the Department of Philosophy at the University of Antwerp, for their generous encouragement while I was working on the book.

An economic utopia carries the risk of degeneration into a catastrophe. I stated this thirty years ago in my doctoral dissertation. At that time, I was full of hope that we would be able to keep the frightening chaos at bay. Today, the negative impact of the economy on man, society and the environment has only grown worse. But economic paradigms with relevant answers that are taking root all over the world are restoring my trust. The utopian hope for spaces where a better future might be possible is giving ground, all over the world, to the confidence of taking concrete, economic responsibility.

1. A Letter to the Reader, by way of Introduction

Bhutan was once my name.
That is a place where no one goes.
More's Utopia now I claim
To match, or beat at its own game;
For that was just a myth in prose,
But what I wrote of, I became,
Of men, wealth, laws, a solid frame,
A place where every wise man goes:
Bheutan, land of happiness, is now my name.[1]

Dear reader,

May I write you a letter, just as Thomas More wrote to Antwerp city official Pieter Gillis by way of an introduction to his *Utopia*? May I propose that I take you on an imagined tour to the foot of Antwerp's cathedral, where you see me talking with a vaguely familiar person who is employed by the mayor's office in the nearby City Hall? You bought the book that is now lying in front of you, maybe because you were somewhat intrigued by its title: *The Economy and Meaningfulness. A Utopia?* You're presuming that it might very well deal with the possibility of meaningfulness in the economy. Not so much with meaningfulness in terms of the desire, or striving, of an economy to earn lots of money, but maybe rather with the meaningfulness that the economy can have for people. And this is probably linked to the meaningfulness of your own life, or of life itself, in the midst of economic activity. Meanwhile, you read in the dictionary that *meaningfulness* should be understood as the search for the sense, the aim, or the usefulness of life.

1 This is a slightly altered version of the poem at the beginning of More's *Utopia*, directly preceding his letter to Pieter Gillis, in which I've replaced *Utopia, Eutopia* and Plato with Bhutan, Bheutan and More's Utopia. The original poem plays on the words Utopia (a place that does not exist) and Eutopia (a place of happiness).

You see me talking with this person and, as you are now carrying this book, you are invited to join me for lunch along with my conversation partner. You learn that I have just returned from a conference in Bhutan, a tiny Buddhist microstate in the Himalayas, about the size of Switzerland, with a population of just over 750,000. And the longer you hear me talking with this man, the more you become interested in the topic, while at the same time you have serious doubts about the economic feasibility of that Bhutanese model, one that is based on *Gross National Happiness* instead of *Gross National Product*. In my story, you notice fragments from a different book: *Utopia*, by Thomas More. Maybe you, yourself, are a person with some degree of social responsibility, not unlike Thomas More, the Under-Sheriff of London.

To be honest, I hesitated before deciding to publish this book. So much has already been written on utopia in commemoration of the publication of More's *Utopia*. It might be better *not to worry oneself*[2] by publishing a book that one hopes *people will find amusing, or useful, despite their lofty criticism. Most readers know nothing about literature; many even regard it with contempt. Lowbrows find everything that is not outright banal too difficult, and intellectuals find everything banal that is not full of difficult words.*[3], However, the very fact that the global wealth of the richest 1 per cent of the world population exceeds that of the remaining 99 per cent[4] forces me to take a stand: *Maybe you think that a society is just if all the beautiful things of life are reserved for those who least deserve them, or are happy if everything is divided among a handful of people who are not satisfied even then, while the rest*

2 When I paraphrase Thomas Morus, always printed in italics and based on the translation of Morus (2014), I often replace the term "Utopians" with "they" or "him", to facilitate the comparison with Bhutan. In footnotes I often refer to other translations of Morus' *Utopia*.

3 "Nevertheless, to tell the truth, I have not yet made up my own mind whether or not to publish this. So varied are the tastes of mortals, so peevish the characters … Many are ignorant of learning; many despise it. The barbarian rejects as harsh whatever is not utterly barbarian. Those with pretensions to learning despise as trite whatever is not packed with obsolete expressions" (More, 2010, 26).

4 *Richest 1 per cent will own more than all the rest by 2016* (Oxfam, 2015). Source: https://www.oxfam.org/en/pressroom/pressreleases/2015-01-19/richest-1-will-own-more-all-rest-2016

are very unhappy. I do not think so.[5] Surely, we cannot think so when we see so many modern refugees, and we notice how many of our utopian economic projects, as well as our environment and climate, are increasingly being destroyed. You almost hear me saying to this man: *Your sheep, who used to be so tame and were always content with so little food, have now become so voracious, so unstoppable, that they say that they are going to devour the people themselves, their fields and houses and villages everywhere … In their eyes, the lease and the age-old yield of their land were not enough any more, at least not enough to maintain their selfish, unproductive, extravagant lifestyle, while at the same time they totally ignored the common interest, or worse, damaged it. So now they are confiscating all the fields, and putting fences around their pastures. Poor people are forced to leave – men, women, couples, windows, and orphans, parents with small children are all forced to leave, I say, from their known and familiar homes, with nowhere else to go.*[6]

As I happened to bump into this politician, with his important networks that reach into Brussels and across the globe, I seized my chance: *Put an end to this sick situation! Decree that those who destroyed your farms and villages have to rebuild them, or hand them over to the people who are willing to replace and rebuild them. Prevent the rich from their practices of buying everything up, from their monopolistic freedom*

---

5 Maybe you think "that justice is there executed where all things come into the hands of evil men, or that prosperity there flourisheth where all is divided among a few, which few nevertheless do not lead their lives very wealthily, and the residue live miserably, wretchedly, and beggarly" (More, 1912, 130).

6 "Your sheep that were wont to be so meek and tame, and so small eaters, now, as I heard say, be become so great devourers and so wild, that they eat up, and swallow down the very men themselves. They consume, destroy, and devour whole fields, houses, and cities. For look in what parts of the realm doth grow the finest, and therefore dearest wool, there noble men, and gentlemen, yea and certain Abbots, holy men no doubt, not contenting themselves with the yearly revenues and profits, that were wont to grow to their forefathers and predecessors of their lands, nor being content that they live in rest and pleasure nothing profiting, yea much noying [injuring] the weal public, leave no ground for tillage: they inclose all into pastures, they throw down houses, they pluck down towns, and leave nothing standing, but only the church to be made a sheephouse. And as though you lost no small quantity of ground by forests, chases, lawns, and parks, those good holy men turn all dwelling places and all glebe land into desolation and wilderness" (1912, 90).

of trade.[7] I address his common-sense, conservative reflex to restore virtues: *When you allow people to be raised without values and their character is ruined from an early age, and you only begin to intervene when they commit the crimes in adulthood, what are you doing if not turning them into thieves and then punishing them after the fact?*[8] But when I say *what I think it all boils down to – that in no place where private property exists and where money is the measure of all things may we talk of a just or prosperous society,*[9] you, the reader, would frown as well. You'd probably say that you don't agree with me and say: *I do not think that a pleasant life is possible in a society with nothing but common property.*[10] The man would emphatically state that an alternative economic system isn't our cup of tea – *unless you want to drag the country to the edge of the abyss.*[11] I can hear you saying: As you have returned from Bhutan, it is about time that you give us a description of that land. *Take plenty of time for this: the land, the water, the cities, the people, society, the structures of the state, the legislative system, and everything else you think we might be interested in.*[12]

Thus, I would start talking enthusiastically about Bhutan, the country where I was invited to deliver a paper in the fall of 2015, at the International Conference on Gross National Happiness.[13]

---

7 "Cast out these pernicious abominations. Make a law that they which plucked down farms and towns of husbandry shall build them up again or else yield and uprender the possession of them to such as will go to the cost of building them anew. Suffer not these rich men to buy up all, to engross and forestall, and please them" (1912, 94).

8 "For if you suffer your people to be ill-educated, and their manners to be corrupted from their infancy, and then punish them for those crimes to which their first education disposed them, what else is to be concluded from this, but that you first make thieves and then punish them?" (More, 1737, 17).

9 "… it seems to me that wherever there is private property, where everything is measured in terms of money, it is hardly ever possible for the common good to be served with justice and prosperity" (2010, 55).

10 "It seems to me that men cannot live conveniently where all things are common" (1737, 41).

11 "… they lead their country by a short route to chaos." Source: https://www.thomasmoresociety.org/about/sir-thomas-more/

12 In what follows I go more deeply into these topics.

13 *Provisional Findings of 2015 Gross National Happiness Survey,* Centre for Bhutan Studies & GNH Research, Timphu, ISBN 978-99936 – 14-80-08, 2015.

I can recall the essence of that country by continuing to browse through Thomas More's *Utopia* and telling you stories of Bhutan, in the same way that Raffaello glowingly reports to More about Utopia in the second book. Just the arrival at the small airport near the capital city of Timphu, where there is only one airstrip, has something special. A short while earlier, you were flying close to the Himalayas, with Mount Everest, and you concluded that this country has indeed been well protected for centuries in the midst of those mountains: *Everywhere, the passage to the hinterland … is so well protected that a handful of trained coastguards is enough to stop an army.*[14] And when you travel across the country, you are quickly struck by the fact that in every city you encounter a fair degree of uniformity: *As much as the natural location allows it, their design and appearance are the same everywhere.*[15] Or: *They are so much alike that when you know one city, you know them all.*[16] Every one of these identical towns, however, is surrounded by splendid agricultural land. The available land is divided among the cities in such an efficient way that *the available land is so efficiently divided among the cities that each city governs at least twenty square miles of agricultural land surrounding it.*[17]

Throughout its history, although it has been invaded several times by Tibet, India and Nepal, Bhutan has almost never been successfully *occupied* by foreign peoples, nor was Bhutan itself keen on expanding its territory: its people live far from the sea and their country is surrounded by mountains on almost all sides. Because they are perfectly satisfied with the yield of their land, there is very little trade with other peoples.[18] *For centuries, they have felt no need to expand their territory,*[19] *because the natural borders they have, thanks to the mountains, and the tribute they pay to their protector, keep them*

---

14 "So fortified, both by nature and art, that a small number of men can hinder the descent of a great army" (1737, 45).

15 "The manners, customs, and laws of all their cities are the same, and they are all contrived as near in the same manner as the ground on which they stand will allow" (ibid.).

16 "He that knows one of their towns knows them all" (1737, 48).

17 "Every city has so much ground set off for its jurisdiction, that there is twenty miles of soil round it, assigned to it" (1737, 46).

18 With the notable exception of India.

19 With a few exceptions.

safe from invasion.[20] The exception to this in Bhutan is the presence of "strongholds", called *dzongs,*[21] in all major cities. These fortresses were erected from the seventeenth century onward, when Tibet regularly invaded the country.

Their lives are not luxurious, though they are rather pleasant and with decent prosperity., Their country does not play a conspicuous role in the world.[22] *For that reason, except their immediate neighbours, only a few people have heard of them.*[23] What is striking is the overwhelming presence of pictures of the present and past kings of Bhutan, in the streets and on houses and buildings. The king is extremely popular.[24]

It was the previous king, Jigme Singye Wangchuck, now in his sixties, who created the idea of *Gross National Happiness* – often the very reason that people in faraway places first heard of Bhutan. In 1972, a journalist pointed out to the king that Bhutan scored relatively low in terms of Gross National Product. Upon hearing this, the king promptly answered that there is also something such as happiness in people's lives, and that too much desire for production might very well endanger that happiness. It was as if the king had read the 1972 report from the Club of Rome, *The Limits to Growth,*[25] in which, for the first time, several serious intellectuals used a model of economic and population growth to simulate the consequences of interactions between Earth's and human systems. Could Plato have been right

---

20 "They lie far from the sea, and are environed with hills; and being contented with the productions of their own country, which is very fruitful, have little commerce with any other nation. According to the genius of their country, they have no inclination to enlarge their borders; and their mountains, and the pension they pay to the Persian, secure them from invasion" (1737, 20).

21 *Dzongs*: fortresses, mainly in Bhutan and Tibet, known for their distinct, massive style and towering exterior walls that surround a complex of temples, administrative offices and monks' quarters.

22 Except for the fame garnered from having the *Gross National Happiness* index.

23 "Their lives are not luxurious, though rather pleasant with a high degree of welfare. Their country does not play a conspicuous role in the world. Beyond their neighbors across the border, only few people have heard of them" (2014, 42).

24 In a parallel, in the Afterword to the Dutch translation of *Utopia* (2014, 167), Marja Brouwers states that, however explicitly Utopia may be a republic, the untouchable status of the monarchy "could not have been a matter of doubt" to a magistrate such as More.

25 Meadows (1972).

when he said that for a "beautiful city" like Kallipolis – a utopia – to come into being, *philosophers [must] rule as kings, or those now called kings [must] genuinely and adequately philosophize?*

Almost everyone in Bhutan owns a house and a piece of agricultural land. If necessary, the king will give you a piece of land and a dwelling. In fact, *nobody owns a house that is just his ... And these days, they have impressive houses with three storeys.*[26] The ground floor is always reserved for the animals, with strikingly peaceful dogs that make a loud racket at night only occasionally. *Beyond agriculture (in which, as I said, everyone is already adept) everyone has to learn one additional skill. Most of the time, this is the processing of wool or linen.*[27] A result of this is that you see people wearing the same kind of brightly coloured[28] clothing: *Everywhere, people wear largely the same kinds of clothes, except for differences between the sexes.*[29]

It is remarkable that the working hours are not excessively long, but that there are no essential shortages. Because they *work only six hours a day, you might expect a shortage of all kinds of necessary goods. But that is not the case at all, because six hours is not only sufficient to produce everything they need to stay alive and make life pleasant, there is even time left!*[30] Obviously, this is a product of guaranteeing the Gross National Happiness. *For the authorities refuse to force people to do unnecessary work against their will, as the whole organization of society serves only one purpose, that is to free people from physical labour, insofar as the general welfare permits, so that they can devote as much time as possible to the free development of their spirit. For here lies, according to them, the key*

---

26 "But now all the houses are handsome, with three stories and walls faced by flint, plaster, or brick"(More, 2010, 64).

27 "Besides agriculture, which as I said is common to all, each person is taught some craft, generally wool working, preparing linen, masonry, carpentry, blacksmith's work, or silk weaving" (2010, 65).

28 In *Utopia,* in contrast to Bhutan, all the clothes are the same colour: "When they go outdoors they put on a cloak to hide their working clothes; all over the island, this garment has the same natural color" (2010, 69).

29 "Each family makes its own clothes, which are in the same style throughout the island except for distinctions between the sexes and between the married and the single" (2010, 65).

30 "Since Utopians spend only six hours working, you might think that some scarcity of goods must follow. But this is far from the case: the time is more than ample to supply a wealth of necessities, even of conveniences" (2010, 67).

to a happy life.[31] That is why, in Bhutan, they develop the technology for agriculture or weaving in such a way as to avoid the unnecessarily heavy physical labour, without making it so numbing that it would thwart the happy development of the spirit. There is an important debate within Bhutan questioning whether such a balanced system of labour would be possible without the contribution of foreign labour, *hard-working poor labourers from other countries,*[32] working in Bhutan. At times, some question the formal attitude of Bhutan's authorities to foreign workers, mostly from Nepal: *They treat these people with respect and almost as well as their own citizens, although they do give them a little more work, to which they are already accustomed.*[33]

The reason why relatively few people go to Bhutan – as was mentioned in the opening lines of the poem at the beginning of this Introduction – might not so much be because Bhutan is not as cheap as the average tourist destination in the East, as because you are normally required to be accompanied by an experienced local guide. *So, because you cannot just wander around, there is never an acceptable reason for doing nothing. There are no wine bars, no pubs, no brothels, no opportunities for misbehaviour, no secret places, and no closed meetings. On the contrary, the all-seeing eye of your surroundings makes it imperative for you to stay busy with your normal work and not behave indecently in your free time.*[34] Thus, you'll never bump into *poor people or beggars,* and *it is deemed disgraceful to mock someone for a disability.*[35] *The whole country is, as it*

[31] "For they do not keep the citizens against their will at unnecessary labor. The constitution of the commonwealth has one objective: that so far as public needs permit, as much time as possible should be taken from serving the body and devoted to the freedom and cultivation of the mind. In that, they believe, consists the happiness of life" (2010, 69).

[32] "Poor laborers in other countries who voluntarily exchange their drudgery for slavery in Utopia" (2010, 92).

[33] "Except for having somewhat more work assigned to them, these are treated almost as well as are citizens" (ibid.).

[34] "So you can see that there is no way of evading work and no pretext for idleness: no wine shop, no ale house, no brothel, no occasion for depravity, no lurking holes, no secret meetings. Everything is open to everyone, and everyone is bound either to do the usual work or to take lawful and not indecent recreation" (2010, 74).

[35] "To mock someone for a deformity or the loss of a limb they think shames the mocker, not the one mocked; it is stupid to find fault with something not in our power to avoid" (2010, 95).

were, one big family.[36] *Everyone who comes to that country as a tourist and can teach them something, or has seen a lot of the world, is welcomed with open arms. That is why we received such a warm welcome, because it is no exaggeration to say that they are really eager to hear about what is happening around the world.*[37] Indeed, the contact I had with colleagues and students there, before and after my lecture, was heartwarming.

In their schools, they usually start learning English at age fourteen, *as it commands a large vocabulary, is pleasant to the ear, and is one of the most trusted means of expressing one's thoughts. What's more, it has spread almost everywhere.*[38] Especially if the goal is to make the concept of *Gross National Happiness* famous worldwide, being fluent in a widely spoken language – a *lingua franca* like *their own* in *Utopia*, or English in today's world – is an enormous advantage. *Apart from the fact that they have effortlessly mastered the new writing and pronounced the words fluently, they also knew how to learn everything by heart so fast that we could hardly believe what we saw.*[39]

Furthermore, besides the loyalty the Bhutanese have for their king, their self-evident faith in Buddhism is striking. It is, therefore, not surprising that in Bhutan, *no other office outside that of the king is esteemed as highly* as that of the Buddhist monk. What's more, even though there is no emphasis on the separation of church and state, they have succeeded rather well in containing the abuse of power by religious leaders: *it is the task of the head of state and other authorities to confront offenders with their behaviour and to punish them.* In every conversation that is held in Bhutan *about human happiness they combine starting points that they borrow from religion with rational arguments from philosophy. For they are convinced that human reason is not sufficient*

---

36 "Thus the whole island is like a single family" (2010, 75).

37 "I am sure there is none of them to whom you would not be very welcome, for you are capable not only of entertaining a ruler with this learning and experience of countries and people, but also of furnishing him with examples and assisting him with counsel" (2010, 77).

38 "For it is rich in vocabulary, pleasing to the ear, and well adapted for expressing thought. Much of that part of the world has the same language, though sometimes in a variety of corrupted forms" (2010, 79).

39 "They began so easily to imitate the shapes of the letters, so readily to pronounce the words, so quickly to learn by heart, and so faithfully to reproduce what they learned, that it would have seemed a miracle" (2010, 89).

and too limited for the search for authentic happiness. In this, they are very close to the stoic vision of happiness, meaning that *in their eyes, we are good people when we are living according to our nature.*[40] At the same time, *our reason and our common sense also make it clear that we should lead our lives with as little fear and as much joy as possible, and that we should help others do the same out of solidarity.*[41] Especially when, in the book in front of you, we'll discover that fear is proven to be the engine of an economy that unilaterally seeks the growth of the Gross National Product, whereas joy constitutes the heart of an economy where happiness is central, this Buddhist philosophy of compassion will prove to be crucial. In the final section of *Utopia*, anguish and happiness occupy centre stage. Just as in Bhutan today, *no one ought to fear that any person will ever lack anything: everyone gets more than enough, so there is no poverty there and nobody is forced to beg. Never fear that there will be nothing to eat – there will always be enough to live and be happy.*[42] As we shall see, a key element in this is the abolition of pride. *For pride's measure of prosperity is not what you have, but what others don't have. This fault is too deeply ingrained in human nature to be easily eradicated.*[43]

At the end of this letter, dear reader, I'll bid you adieu the way Thomas More did at the end of his letter to Antwerp city official Pieter Gillis, at the beginning of his *Utopia*:

Greetings and best wishes. Like me, never forget our friendship.[44]

And can you imagine better friends than those who are already mutually interested in economy and meaningfulness …?

---

40 "By pleasure they understand every activity or state of body or mind in which a person delights under the guidance of nature" (2010, 83).

41 "Reason urges and admonishes us to lead lives as free from care and as full of joy as possible, and, because of our natural fellowship, to help others do likewise" (2010, 80).

42 "No one fears not having enough, provided the common warehouses are well filled. The distribution of good things is not ungenerous, and there are no poor people or beggars: though nobody can have just anything he wants, everyone is rich" (2010, 116).

43 "For pride measures prosperity not by her own good but by the harm of others … Pride is too deeply rooted in us to be readily plucked out" (2010, 118).

44 "Love me as you have ever done, for I love you more than ever" (2010, 27).

2. Dystopia vs Utopia

The Economy is Sinking, Long Live the Economy[45]

"The economy is sinking, long live the economy" – a succinct summary of the way today's economy is perceived. Venturing out further and further onto high seas risks capsizing the ship of economy. You might think first of ecological problems, but the saying could just as well refer to the dissatisfaction of people on shop floors, or to the increasing socio-economic inequality between rich and poor. It's not long before we try to express this in terms of money, the chosen metaphor for what we conceive as the heart of the economy. "Money does not make people happy", as the renowned economist Richard Layard (2005) of the London School of Economics summarized it. Layard and others, in exploring the concept of *Happiness Economics*, often refer to the concept of *Gross National Happiness* (GNH) that Bhutan invented and developed in its own kingdom. We can applaud an economy just as much when it effectively focuses on the happiness of its people instead of just trying to turn one dollar into two, the primary measure of a Gross National Product (GNP). A question that will appear in this book is whether countries such as Norway, Luxemburg and the Netherlands prove effectively that money does make us happy. For in these countries, at first sight, we see the development of a kind of dialectical synthesis between an economy aimed at increasing its Gross National Product and an economy aimed at producing more Gross National Happiness. It's not for nothing that Angus Deaton, winner of the 2015 Nobel Prize for Economics, initially developed theories simply to measure poverty and track increases in consumption, but later also focused at least as much on health, respect for nature and happiness. The outline of a

---

45 Headline in the Flemish newspaper *De Standaard*, 25 November 2013. Like the twentieth-century philosopher Ernst Bloch, I will occasionally refer to what Bloch called "tracks" or "trailheads" – news clips, media or political events.

sustainable economy begins to emerge, with, among other features, a work environment where constructive co-operation becomes possible, alongside competition. Nature is turned into a partner. The reduction of the economic inequality between people becomes a possibility. We see how the idea of *Gross National Happiness* – from Bhutan's King Singye Wangchuck – has been evolving, since 1973, into an economic theory, and making its way to other countries. And now it has also been affirmed as a "fundamental human goal" by the United Nations.[46] Indeed, it is the UN Millennium initiative that established formal Sustainable Development Goals (SDGs)[47] which are attempting to translate this happiness into economic terms (see Chapter 5).

Did this breakthrough of the idea of sustainability reach a new peak in 2015, when, on the eve of the great Climate Conference in Paris, world leaders at the United Nations invited Pope Francis to attend? – not so much because he was a man who is universally respected, but even more perhaps because, by acting thus, the countries of the world together prompted the Pope to strike a blow for an economy of compassion – compassion towards people and towards nature – at the beginning of the Vatican's Jubilee of Mercy? We'll return to this compassion later. However, the present trend towards an economy that produces happiness has been seriously reinforced by the idea of what evolutionary biologists, such as E. O. Wilson, now call *eusociality*.[48]

The evolutionary advantage of a responsible global approach to social and ecological sustainability problems might very well take us further than we can realize through only individual altruism towards our next of kin. At first sight, it doesn't even seem necessary to mention compassion, as Pope Francis did at the United Nations, in order to magically transform the ship of the economy into a happiness cruise. As nature is constantly reshuffling itself in order to secure its survival, to paraphrase philosopher Slavoj Žižek, the governing bodies of our society seem to have finally understood that they'll have to take nature into account.

---

46 Source: https://www.un.org/apps/news/story.asp?NewsID=39084

47 Source: http://www.undp.org/content/undp/en/home/sustainable-development-goals.html

48 Source: http://www.nature.com/nature/journal/v466/n7310/full/nature09205.html

Realized Instead of Imaginary

The Greek stem *eu-* ("good, real, happy") in the word *eusociality* takes us straight to the better-known term *utopia*. It is remarkable how the word *utopia* is all too quickly and condescendingly dismissed as the naively impossible. This connects us to the other Greek stem, of *ou-* (a negation). Thus, a utopia becomes indeed an impossibility, through being a non-existing topos or site. One can look down in the same way upon the phenomenon of eusociality, from the supremacy of an individualistic culture that only acknowledges Darwin's *struggle for life*. However, five hundred years ago (in 1516), Thomas More wrote his *Utopia* on the occasion of his encounter with his Flemish friend Pieter Gillis in Antwerp, a story in which an imaginary good and happy society is described. Here he is questioning an unacceptably high inequality, a unilateral private property and a war economy. This essay in political philosophy is part of a tradition of utopian writings such as Plato's *Republic* (380 BCE), Francis Bacon's *The New Atlantis* (1627), Charles Fourier's *Le nouveau monde* (1829) and Aldous Huxley's *Island* (1962), all the way up to Michel Houellebecq's *La possibilité d'une île* (2005). In each example, we are dealing with the imaginary description of a happy society, often in a small kingdom, such as Bhutan today, or on a small island. When we try to apply these ideas concretely, things often appear to go wrong. Think of Plato's failed attempt to establish such a commune on the island of Sicily, not far from Lampedusa, where today foreigners would come to seek their utopian happiness. And of Bhutan's government, which has also earned some criticism. And notwithstanding Marx's fierce criticism of those he called "utopian socialists", the demise of communism puts him in similar territory – that of a theory that was impossible to realize in practice.

And so we arrive at the opposite of the concept of utopia: dystopia. Here we encounter the Greek stem *dus-* or *dys-* ("*bad*"). Rather than entering a happy society, we end up in a dystopia, a place with deeply negative traits – imagine the negative effects of the economy we mentioned earlier, such as a polluted environment and inequality. The most frequently cited example of dystopia is George Orwell's 1949 novel, *Nineteen Eighty-Four*, aka *1984*. Other examples include *Brave New World* (1932) by Aldous Huxley and *Lord of the Flies* (1954) by William Golding, alongside contemporary works like *Happy Slaves*

(2013) by Tom Lanoye and *Soumission* (*Submission*, 2015) by Michel Houellebecq. Individual freedom (such as autonomy on the job) is thwarted, emotionality is dislodged by calculated rationality (burnout problems), and man is turned into a means (cf. "human *resource* management") instead of the focus, the goal (cf. "the human person").

It is very important to point out at the beginning of this book that, when I talk about utopia or dystopia, I am not thinking of *imaginary* but, as Hans Achterhuis (2006, 52) puts it, actually *realized* positive and negative situations: "I have already said that our modern society contains some traits of a realized utopia. This appears to be the case with dystopia, as well." Thus our (albeit threatened) welfare state is a positive realization of what More depicted embryonically in *Utopia*. That our privacy is more and more besieged by modern technology was already described as "Big Brother" in Orwell's dystopian *1984*. Another example is: on the one hand, the positive breakthrough of the ecological movement, and, on the other, the negative weight of bureaucracy. And in the foreword to *The Limits of the Green Economy* (2017), the authors also speak in terms of a *realized* utopia/dystopia when they state that the assembled elites continue undisturbed, realizing their collective phantasmagorical utopia. Those who are bothered by the use of terms such as "dystopia" and "utopia" are of course free to use what in economic terms[49] are called "negative and positive external effects". That way, however, we run the risk of getting stuck in the literature of the 1970s and the 80s about the contradiction between economic welfare and well-being. In that literature, they talk at most about a potentially necessary ethical component of the economy.

The need to include *meaningfulness* in the economy equally, the case made in this book, was all but absent at that time. As we have already seen, both dystopia and utopia deal with aspects of meaningfulness such as anguish, suffering, hope, and longing for sustainable happiness. Because, as we shall elaborate on later, the emergence of the economy is related to elements such as fear and desire, it is necessary to refer to "dystopia" and "utopia" to explain extreme developments in the

[49] Joseph Stiglitz, the 2002 Nobel laureate in Economics, talks about a "perverse economy". In his book *Rewriting the Rules of the American Economy: An Agenda for Growth and Shared Prosperity* (2015), he also calls the sum total of potentially positive effects of the economy "shared welfare".

economy. Hence, the use by Achterhuis and others of these terms within an economic context is appropriate.

Equally important for a clear future understanding of terms such as "utopian" and "dystopian" in an economic context is the fact that these are subjectively loaded terms. For neoliberals, for example, the "free market" implies a positively valued utopian context that we should potentially strive for, while from the perspective of the environment or the phenomenon of inequality, that free market can just as well be described as a *dystopian* context. Achterhuis (2006, 37) refers here to the French philosopher Jean Baudrillard, who described the USA as a realized utopia, but adds: "It is precisely in America that Europeans often perceive dystopian traits."[50]

Finally, we're also about to discover in the following pages that, simply from a strictly economic perspective, we need a new interpretation of what we usually call "utopia". As early as the eighteenth century, utopias stopped placing the better living conditions that one dreamt of at a specific geographical site (or *topos*, Greek for "common place"). They increasingly started to be situated in the future. We don't really so much need visions of the future that are often impossible to realize, but rather the concrete and sustained development of socioeconomic improvements. Today, such initiatives are certainly taking place in specific locations all over the world, but at the same time, they take the threats to our globalized society seriously as well.

In summary, it comes down to the fact that our society, in which the economy has become a hugely determining factor, is saddled with the ambiguity between dystopia and utopia. "The economy is sinking, long live the economy" encapsulates this tension well. On the one hand, we firmly associate unfortunate external effects, or dystopia, with the economy. On the other, we witness breakthrough after breakthrough in economic happiness, despite all the talk of doom, as though people around the world are working tangibly on a concrete utopia of happy fellowship. Aaron Hurst (2014, 7, 19), author of *The Purpose Economy*, states that we should not regard the economy of meaningfulness and purpose that society seeks as a blueprint, but as a realistic *work in progress*. "It may sound utopian, but there is evidence

---

50 Achterhuis (2010, 37).

in almost every industry and throughout our culture that this shift is already underway" (2014, 32).[51] The foreword to *The Limits of the Green Economy* (2017) mentioned above explains how the social-ecological utopia is not a pipe dream but an acute necessity.[52]

Fear vs Hope

Gradually, we'll discover that behind dystopia and utopia, the two apparently irreconcilable tendencies in our perception of the economy, two key concepts are hidden. For an economy that is confronted too often with its negative effects (dystopia) turns out to have deep roots in phenomena such as *fear*. It is no accident that Hobbes writes at the beginning of his *Leviathan:* "Fear and I are twins." But an economy in which a happy society prevails depends upon the equally essential phenomenon of *hope*. In his book *Shift: A User's Guide to the New Economy*, Haydn Shaughnessy (2015, 337) summarizes the tension between fear and hope into two perspectives, and instead of *fear* he uses the much rarer term *angst* (anguish), a nod to the particularly intense feeling of *anguish* that Hobbes described as well: "There are two views of the Western economy. On one side there is angst over the way the large firms behave ... On the other side, there is some optimism that a new commons-based economy, or collaborative economy (or sharing economy) is rewriting the rules of wealth creation and distribution."

It will be an important question whether and how we will prevail over fear, if we hope to transcend dystopia. Think of Nelson Mandela's famous saying: "May your choices reflect your hopes, not your fears." Slavoj Žižek argues that *desire*, more than hope, contains the primal force with the potential to free oneself from fear.[53] We may even include here the strongest form of dystopia, death. As another atheist philosopher, Luc Ferry, aptly elaborates throughout his *Apprendre à vivre* ("*Learning to Live*", 2006), we're not merely terribly afraid of death. Death invokes intense desire as well. Believers, such as in the

---

51 In his Humanisme Intégral (1936), the personalist Jacques Maritain argues that this process is never completed. The definitive equilibrium is never reached; one is always "on the way", in motion.

52 Kenis (2017), p. ix.

53 https://www.groene.nl/artikel/noorwegen-bestaat-niet

music of Bach, often speak of a desire for a life after death, one in which we'll be reunited with our loved ones. Towards the end of his book, Ferry talks about his empathy with this religious expression, as it says something about the desire with which every human being is imbued. The fact that, in this book, the emphasis is on the search for a concrete utopia – one that places the hope and desire for sustainable happiness above the dystopia that centres on fear and suffering – reflects that same focus. Consider the impetus that drives refugees to leave a country like Syria. It doesn't *just* involve the fear of death in their own country but, at least as strongly, the desire to live.

Trust as Meaningfulness in the Economy

At the moment when, over and above fear and suffering, hope and desire are linked to *trust*, it becomes obvious that the dimension of *meaningfulness behind the economic* is revealed. Central to this book is this evolution from a society that is excessively focused on *economic makeability* to a society that is once again *receptive* to meaningfulness behind the economic. This receptivity expresses itself concretely in one or the other form of trust, the belief that somebody or something can be trusted. It could be trust in an alternative, electronic kind of money, *Bitcoin*, in another person in whose house you rent a room through *Airbnb*, in nature when you support *Fair Trade* products in your consumer choices, or in some other form of transcendence that you, a sustainable entrepreneur, rely upon. Already in 2002, empirical research by Wim Moesen showed that a state where there is a lack of trust does indeed function less harmoniously. When a climate of trust prevails in a country (such as Bhutan or Norway), you decrease unnecessary costs. When people do business together and know that they can trust each other, they're less likely to cheat one another. When companies trust each other, they do not need lawyers to scrutinize their contracts.

Over and above the tension between utopia and dystopia, you notice that in all world views and religions,[54] trust is emerging. It

54 Roger Scruton (2014) argues that, in all religions, we encounter a kind of begging, in which the unknown is implored to reveal itself as the object and subject of love. To search for God is to search for a person who offers redemption, somebody you trust with your life.

is striking that in Christian as well as Jewish, Islamic, Hindu and Buddhist versions of the myth of the end of times, we find utopian *and* dystopian interpretations that deal with themes of fear, suffering, longing and hope. This occurs just as well in secular utopian and dystopian constructs, such as Luc Ferry's (2010) account of the history of the rise of communism through to the fall of the Third Reich. In each case, the dialectical synthesis between utopian and dystopian perspectives is based upon trust. One might think of eschatologies,[55] specifically visions of the end of the world that we find in all religions (Abrahamic and otherwise). In linking Christian[56] eschatologies to utopia, Achterhuis (2006, 29) expresses it this way: "Human beings keep … longing for a totally different reality that transcends our reality. They keep asking questions about death and life, meaningfulness and the future, which utopia will never be able to answer. In eschatology … God has the last word, while in utopia, that is usually up to man." In the previous century, Martin Buber explained how in eschatology, the decisive act comes from above, while in utopia, everything is subordinated to a conscious human will. In eschatology, makeability is not as primordial as it is in classic utopia. One can relate makeability to the famous first two questions of Immanuel Kant: *What can I know?* and *What should I do?*. Theoretically, when human beings answer these questions, there is always the risk of dystopia. Trust, however, evokes Kant's third (receptive) philosophical question: *What may I expect?*. Beyond fear and hope, a concrete form of trust can grow: a trust that can carry man a long way. Call it meaningfulness, in the sense of receiving meaningfulness by letting the other speak, as Levinas formulates it. Thus, the *giving-of-meaningfulness* turns into the *encounter-with-meaningfulness*. This might be the opposite of what we read in the dictionary: that we, as human beings, have to search by ourselves for the meaning, the goal and the usefulness of life. When

---

55 Eschatology: the part of theology concerned with death, judgement and the final destiny of the soul and of humankind.

56 Perhaps paradoxically, the atheist philosopher Maarten Boudry (2015) prefers a religious eschatological version, such as the Christian one, to a communist or ecological one. For a Christian trusts a loving God in an irrational way, but still considers Him a rational creator. According to Boudry, however, it is hard to find a rational basis for a communist or ecological eschatology.

you find meaningfulness within the economic realm, you're receiving keys to the meaning of life.

When you are too eager to throw yourself into the economy, it is a sign that this will become the goal of your life, whereas dystopia proves that exactly this behaviour is a threat to your life. Discerning or discovering meaningfulness within the economy teaches you that you can only admit life into the economy again when you relinquish makeability. Certainly, this is not to be understood in an exclusively religious sense, as it is in eschatology, but rather along the lines of Paul Tillich (1952, 164), who writes that the "courage to be is the courage to accept oneself as accepted".[57] You can be yourself and find meaningfulness by entrusting yourself to life and the world around you.

An Actively Pluralistic Economy of Meaningfulness

At first sight, this does not square with the vision expressed a few years ago in an essay called *Zineconomie* (*Economy of Meaningfulness*). In that essay, Meerten ter Borg (2003, 15) considers meaningfulness as "the placing of things in such a way that people have a clue". Instead of the being of God beyond the normal or physical level, as the dictionary describes *transcendence*, for ter Borg, to transcend is "to go beyond the existing frame, to color outside the box, to create new frames" (2003, 15). And: "The most impressive manifestation of this potential for transcendence is the development of technology" (2003, 54). The makeability vision of meaningfulness is summarized in one line: "Meaningfulness is a product. All meaningfulness is produced" (2003, 32). When this is the core of what ter Borg calls the *economy of meaningfulness*, then, to use ter Borg's own words, "people are playing a dangerous game with their meaningfulness" (2003, 69) – a game that might well have driven us to the essence of today's economic dystopia. Fortunately, the author arrives at a more balanced version in the course of his book. He talks about an ontological abandonment (think of what we call fear or "angst") that calls for ontological security: "In order to be able to live, people ought to be able to trust" (2003, 57). This fundamental need for trust creates a tension with the human

57 Tillich (1952, 164).

tendency to permanently exceed the shortcomings of everyday life, which ter Borg, strange as it might sound, calls transcendence. But what he really means here is technical-economic reality. Unlimited transcendence in this sense of technical-economic progress, however, results in problems: “Unfettered transcendence is frightening ... It has to remain within limits” (2003, 58). This reminds us of the above-mentioned contradiction between Gross National Product and Gross National Happiness. Hence, ter Borg rightly concludes that the most important challenge to the economy of meaningfulness has to be found in what he calls the correct “mix of transcendence with ontological security” (2003, 211). In what follows here, we'll call it the relationship between economy and ethics, which in turn involves the tension between dystopia and utopia.

In the present book, we are searching for an actively pluralistic framework, or frame, one within which *receiving meaningfulness* in trust is taking concrete shape in today's economy. This frame is built most robustly when theistic and non-theistic philosophers advocate responsibility as the means of reinforcing this trust. Active pluralism starts from a diversity of origins and opinions, whereby one lives actively according to one's own world view, in a dialogue with, and with respect for, the other. We're not talking here of an equalization of diversity: on the contrary.

Responsibility that is reflected in concrete economic alternatives today is perhaps best summarized in Martin Buber's terms: “We must create here and now the space *now* possible for the thing for which we are striving, so that it may come to fulfilment *then*” (1950, 13). We are immediately presented here with a synthesis of both above-mentioned perspectives, which, according to Achterhuis, have always been part of classical utopian thinking. Some stress that such happiness is in the distant future, but through trust-based responsibility this is happening today. Still others situate happiness in an altogether different space or location. Nowadays, it could be any site on earth. In this way, a new *concrete* utopia emerges beyond the contradiction between utopia and dystopia, as we shall explain. The longing for and hope of utopia, as opposed to the fear and suffering of dystopia, are now linked to trust. As a result, achievable steps are being taken today, everywhere in this world.

From a theistic angle, the transcending of dystopia is mainly motivated by spirituality. From an agnostic or atheistic perspective, this happens through ethics. With trust, however, a new dimension emerges that transcends the difference between spirituality and ethics. Precisely for this reason, a transition in the economy appears to take hold today at diverse sites and in diverse groups around the world. This is probably the reason why Buddhist philosophy and practice are so popular today. For instance, the heart of Buddhist meditation consists in the art of the trustfully letting go of your ego, which is the core of our makeability. Through this letting go, you open yourself up to what is called *the friendly warm light*.[58] The possible answer from this encounter, compassion, reflects responsibility based upon trust.

Utopia and Dystopia in the Novel

In his essay *Houellebecq économiste* (2014), Bernard Maris studies the way this ambivalent tension between utopia and dystopia is present in the novels of Michel Houellebecq. Think of Houellebecq's *La Possibilité d'une île* (*The Possibility of an Island*), as compared to his novel *Soumission* (*Submission*). Good writers like More, Huxley and Houellebecq are often more capable of depicting dystopian and utopian societies than philosophers are. "With writers, especially novelists, we're always in search of a glimpse of the truth about this frightening world in which we are thrown. For they can speak about death, love, catastrophe and happiness, while economists calibrate by quantifying the GNP" (2014, 15–16). Maris refers here to alternative indices of human and sustainable development. In his way, he is talking about the contrast between Gross National Product and Gross National Happiness. "In order to understand life, economists are constantly stripping it of all its pith, love, desire, violence, fear, terror … in the name of the rationality of human behavior. They're organizing a raid to extinguish emotion, [which interrupts] the causal chain" (2014, 16–17).

---

58 I borrow this potential interpretation of Buddhist meditation from Jan Geurtz, a philosopher of science and education who wrote several books on the topic. See for instance *Addicted to Love* (2016).

Here we're clearly colliding with the importance of emotion, as we shall discover in the work of Martha Nussbaum. It is Nussbaum who, working with the Indian economist and philosopher Amartya Sen, started from the important role of emotions to translate the concept of *Gross National Happiness* into that of the *Human Development Index (HDI).*[59] For this United Nations index, just as in Bhutan (see Chapter 5), takes not only quantitative economic growth into account, but also, in equal measure, the quality of democracy, healthcare and education. We can abandon the discussion in which we must choose whether or not to advocate economic growth as the precondition for progress.[60]

Ecological Capital – the Achilles Heel

After the financial-economic crisis of 2008-13, the economist Paul De Grauwe (2015, 20) of the London School of Economics, initially a pro-globalization neo-liberal, became very critical of prevailing economic practices and sciences. In an interview, he states, regarding the current economic dystopia, that the next world catastrophe might well be triggered by an environmental disaster: "The environment is the Achilles heel of capitalism. Such a disaster could destroy capitalism."[61] It is good to know that, according to Nobel Prize winner Paul Krugman, De Grauwe had been one of the few gifted with the insight to foresee the arrival of the crisis of 2008. What is striking now is the fact that De Grauwe (2015) concludes his analysis with the assertion that a new economic paradigm is becoming unavoidable. It is also remarkable that he states that for this new paradigm, we'll have to develop models that take into account utopian as well as dystopian behaviour: "I'm working out a new method for developing macroeconomic models. The existing models all start from rational behavior: people and organizations are assumed to strive for the best. However, irrational behavior, such as optimism and pessimism,

59 See http://hdr.undp.org/en/content/human-development-index-hdi

60 Nearly fifty years ago, the European think thank The Club of Rome was already advocating for the integration of *qualitative as well as quantitative* metrics.

61 A decade earlier, when asked for a solution to environmental destruction resulting from the globalization, he used the same metaphor: "The environment is the Achilles' heel of globalization" (*De Standaard*, 11 Dec. 2006).

also has a real influence on macroeconomics." As we consider these statements by De Grauwe, note that he starts out from the most negative (or dystopian) effects of our economy (environmental crisis, inequality and dissatisfaction in the workplace), and that he identifies environmental crisis as the primordial problem, the reason that a paradigm shift in economic theory and practice has become urgent.

An author like Dirk Holemans continues further along the lines of De Grauwe's point. He says that stressing the centrality of other crucial negative effects of the economy, as Thomas Piketty does in *Capital in the Twenty-First Century* (2014), carries the risk of neglecting the environment, which makes an environmental crisis that threatens capitalism unavoidable. Holemans argues (2015, 43): "The best thing we may wish for ourselves, after reading *Capital in the Twenty-First Century*, is to suggest that Piketty write a new book, about *ecological capital* in the twenty-first century."

What is striking in the pleas of Paul De Grauwe and Dirk Holemans for a new vision of the economy is the fact that they have the courage to state that the theories and practical examples for this have yet to be invented. Holemans states that a book about this topic should finally be written. And De Grauwe concludes: "For the time being, however, we have only small pieces of the puzzle of such a new paradigm." On the following pages, it becomes clear that, since the 1970s, we've gotten more than just the inception of new sustainable economic paradigms,[62] with works from several economists and philosophers such as Hans Achterhuis's *The Realm of Scarcity* (*Het rijk van de schaarste*, 1988), Paul Dumouchel's *The Ambivalence of Scarcity* (*L'ambivalence de la rareté*, 1979), Serge-Christophe Kolm's *The Good Economy. General Reciprocity* (*La bonne économie. La réciprocité générale*, 1984), Peter Koslowski's *Theory of Ethical Economy* (*Prinzipien der ethischen Oekonomie*, 1988), Amartya Sen's *On Ethical Economics* (1987), Ernst Friedrich Schumacher's *Small Is Beautiful* (1973) and Philippe Van Parijs's essay on the question "What is a just society?" (*Qu'est-ce qu'une société juste?*, 1991).

---

62 It was no accident that the title of my philosophical-economic doctoral thesis in 1985 dealt with "polyparadigmatic thinking as a way to approach the problem-oriented crisis in the foundations of economic science". See also Chapter 4.

That is why, for decades now and well into the present, authors such as Christian Arnsperger (2013), Tim Jackson (2009), Tomáš Sedláček (2011) and Geert Noels (2008) have been paying particular attention to ethics within the economy. For example, for several years now in the Netherlands and Belgium, Noels' book *Econoshock 2.0* has been a standard work. It is a book in which a concretely developed sustainability attempts to bridge the gap between economy and ethics. It is striking that Noels, as opposed to De Grauwe, consistently advocates more equilibrium – and "less is more" – over increased investment, not just as a macroeconomic approach to crisis. Noels (2008) promotes frugality[63] on the microeconomic level as well, in accordance with the theory that will increasingly be called the *Economics of Frugality* (Bouckaert, 2008). This *economics of sufficiency* can be compared to visions of sobriety such as More's in the past, Ernst Friedrich Schumacher's in the twentieth century and Tim Jackson's (2009) today. We do not find a clear description of this *economics of sufficiency* in Gunter Pauli's theory of *the Blue Economy* (2010). In general terms, Pauli argues that, against the background of a circular economy, *sustainable abundance* ought to be acceptable. But doesn't he then run the risk of reverting to an economic theory that will still be harmful to the ecological system *in the long run*?

Economy, Ethics and Justice

For decades, the tension between economy-as-dystopia and economy-as-utopia has been explored from the perspective of the *philosophy of economics*. The philosophy of economics deals, among other things, with the ethical aspects of the economy. That opposition – between economy-as-dystopia and economy-as-utopia – can be traced back to the first philosopher of economics, Aristotle, who already addressed these questions in the fourth century BC. He talked about the distinction between *chrematistics* (the art of getting rich, with all the consequences involved) and *oikonomia* (the art of being responsible for our human household). Why seek this distinction

63 Luc Versteylen (1981), one of the people who inspired Geert Noels, frequently advocated more frugality during the 1970s. His appeal was *"Sober maar niet somber"* (*"Sober but not sombre"*).

unless it is to search for equilibrium between an economy in which the primary stress is on growth (with the risk of dystopia) and a (utopian) economy in which *eudaimonia* – the contented state of being happy, healthy and prosperous – prevails? During the same period as Aristotle, Buddhist philosophy also sought to bridge the gap between these two aspirations: on the one hand, the desire for liberation from anxious (material) suffering, and on the other, the human quest for a happy life. The historian Etienne Hauttekeete (2009, 19) explains that, for this reason, Buddhism "has always participated in the historical metamorphoses of the economic and political life of the society in which it was active".

When the philosophy of economics talks of *economy versus ethics*, we may thus start from the tension between dystopia and utopia. The economy does indeed turn out to entail negative effects. What should the answer of ethics then be, lest you choose to neglect man's happiness? Could the suffering – our need for food, clothing, shelter, etc. – from which the economy originates, but which it also aggravates (burnout at the workplace, inequality, pollution of the environment), be corrected through ethics that aspire to preserve human happiness? Aristotle told us of King Midas, whose wish that everything he touch turn to gold unfortunately included his food, which led to his death.

That is why, in Chapter 3, we'll investigate how people have dealt with the tension between economy and ethics, not just since the introduction of formal economic sciences, but since the beginning of philosophy, out of which economics gradually developed. We'll learn how, since Aristotle, the central ethical concept of the economy turns out to be that of justice. In Chapter 4, we'll see that, furthermore, at the beginning of Modernity, as the foundations of present-day economics were being established, justice was also central. For the philosopher of the social contract, Thomas Hobbes, for example, *justice* consists of sticking to social agreements, thereby starting from the assumption of equality. Gradually, we'll see that such contracts, over which the state has a great say, are no longer sufficient to guarantee justice as a bridge between economics and ethics. Hence, for another philosopher of the social contract, Jean-Jacques Rousseau, freedom, rather than fear of suffering, is primary in securing happiness, although he still invites us to take responsibility. For freedom doesn't just lead us to benefactions of the free market that can feel utopian, but also to dystopian side effects such as excessive wealth and income inequality. In Chapter 5, philosophers of responsibility such as Paul Ricœur and Emmanuel Levinas help us to formulate an answer to this ambivalence. Chapter 6 will demonstrate how responsibility takes shape concretely in today's economy.

3. Economics vs Ethics, Compassion and Equality

The Separation of Economics and Ethics

A few days after Volkswagen's "Dieselgate" scandal in the fall of 2015, the cover of a financial weekly read: "He who doesn't commit fraud does not survive." In 1705, shortly before economics separated from philosophy and emerged as its own discipline, Bernard de Mandeville, an Anglo-Dutch philosopher and political economist, made approximately the same statement. The economy can only function efficiently when we do not care about ethics. And it does even better when we put egoism and competition at the centre instead of taking responsibility. Mandeville gave his economic treaty the following significant subtitle: "Vices *privés,* bienfaits *publics*" (*Private* vices, *public* virtues). What we do out of self-interest (for example, raise prices) will eventually turn into a public blessing (say, as a result of surplus revenue through taxes). Assuming responsibility for the *common good* is here replaced by the maximization of your self-interest. As a philosopher of ethics, Adam Smith, the actual founder of economic sciences at the end of the eighteenth century, still tried to make some ethical corrections to the economy. His main work, however, *An Inquiry into the Nature and Causes of the Wealth of Nations* (1776), was unjustly increasingly interpreted as leaning towards an autonomous economic logic, separate from ethics. In the first half of the nineteenth century, John Stuart Mill was a leading advocate of the separation of economy and ethics. The problem of inequality, for example, was kept out of the purview of economics by definition. At the end of the nineteenth century, we notice that the separation of economy and ethics had definitively conquered the field. In the discipline that Léon Walras called "pure economics", there was no room for ethics. Together with Carl Menger, Walras was also one of the great representatives of the neoclassical school of economic sciences. To this day, this school of thinking defines the most important presuppositions of the economy (see also Chapter 6). Menger posited very explicitly that economics was a neutral, value-free science.

The Compatibility of Economics and Ethics

After Adam Smith, Henry Sedgwick, the nineteenth-century English utilitarian philosopher and economist, also entered economics by way of ethical philosophy. He was also in search of the compatibility between economics and ethics. In that pursuit, he worked out the ethical aspects of the distribution of income. At the end of the nineteenth century, Alfred Marshall attempted to continue developing economic theory along these lines. Among other topics, he dealt with the importance of virtues such as honesty, and the aforementioned trust in doing business. Nor did his students – Arthur Pigou, John Maynard Keynes and Joan Robinson – ignore the ethical component of the economy. Pigou looked at the economy in the service of greater human well-being. Keynes described economics as an ethical science. Robinson clearly indicated that economics is not a "pure science", but is, on the contrary, permeated with ethical values. And the post-Keynesian school that still holds sway today explicitly states that economic science must give ethical aspects their due attention. In addition to these post-Keynesian theories, there are several other economic theories being developed today that integrate ethics. For example, game theory emphasizes that you can only speak of mutual trust when you have included such virtues as integrity and honesty. The core of Mandeville's starting point ("private vices lead to public virtues") is undoubtedly being put to the question here.

From Reason to Instrumental Rationality

It is, however, conspicuous that most of the economic theories that include ethical components in fact still accept the presuppositions of the existing economic paradigm (see also Chapter 6). In this paradigm (a summary of accepted economic theories and presuppositions), from the beginning instrumental rationality has predominated over what we understand as reason and reasonableness. In this, the economic theories followed the natural sciences, which were already quite advanced by that time. In the dictionary, the first meaning of reasonableness is often justice (fairness). It is explained that reasonableness means being capable of reason and being governed by reason or sound thinking, that is, having the ability to *conceive and distinguish*, an ability that is common to all healthy persons. The meaning of justice as a central concept in the ethics of the economy will be linked to this: to grant others what they're entitled to. Or, to put it in plain terms: reason could thus be understood as "common sense". However, *rationality* will become predominant in economics, and *reason* will become subservient to it. Even on those occasions when the economic theories cited above make room for reasonableness, it is in the service of (economic) rationality in most cases. In this way, we can see how the tension between dystopia and utopia – which we have seen linked to the tension between economy and ethics – eventually refers to the tension between rationality and reason.

Today, when we wish to transcend the tension between dystopia and utopia, it is good to realize that their roots are connected to the tension between rationality and reason. Instrumental rationality evolved in the sixteenth and seventeenth centuries, from the broader ethical context of *reasonableness*. Thomas Hobbes wrote his book *Leviathan* in 1651, a time when unilateral rationality was beginning to intrude (see Chapter 4). Leszek Kołakowski, the Polish philosopher, characterizes (premodern) reasonableness starting from a preset natural order and directed at the real living environment. As he frames it, modern rationality, on the contrary, starts from the separation between fact and value, and is abstractly directed at reality. The transition from ethical reason to rationality was thus colluding with a changed conception of nature. It is no surprise then that, according to De Grauwe, the ecologically urgent transition from an overly rational (dystopian) economy to a more reasonable economy breaks through at the very moment when nature is once again threatened. Think of climate change – even today, different conceptions of nature are emerging. Thus, we are speaking today more of the Anthropocene[64] than of the Holocene epoch. It looks as if man is intruding on the logic of nature instead of respecting it. Premodern philosophers

[64] Anthropocene: a proposed epoch dating from the commencement of significant human impact on the Earth's geology and ecosystems.

still looked at nature in the same way as Aristotle had done, that is to say by referring to a *telos*, an ideal model of human endeavour. Modern philosophers, however, turned the concept of nature upside down. Rather than being determined ideally and ethically, it was now determined empirically and psychologically. This meant that nature contained the raw factuality of a natural instinctive life, with an increasing appetite for lust, power and self-preservation (Kolakowski, 2001). In the following chapters, we'll see exactly how the starting point of this instinctive life will lead us, along with Galileo Galilei, to give movement a prominent place and, as a result, to focus on (economic) growth. Today, however, this framework, which has been corroborated by the theory of evolution, will be questioned again, among other things by what biologists are calling *eusociality*.

According to the Belgian philosopher Herman De Dijn, acting along the lines of instrumental *rationality* means that you are consciously and willingly directed at a malleable goal. The *means* are consciously chosen in the service of a well-defined *aim*, such as the maximization of profit (Parret, 1989, 112). Ethical *reasonableness*, by contrast, appeals to fundamental values and longings such as happiness, hope and suffering. For the most part these transcend rationality (Parret, 1989, 4). Reasonable acts are not means to reach autonomous goals, but are rather like goals themselves – in the words of Alasdair MacIntyre, "*goods internal to a practice*" (1981, 175). For Adam Smith, the pursuit of such goals was typical for man. According to Smith, man is more than just a "creature of needs" that is intent on satisfying specific "natural" needs as economically as possible (Parret, 121). Besides, the subject is not the ultimate measure by which to judge the result. There is a principled intention calibrated on the judgement of others (the *other*). We will see more of this with Paul Ricœur and Emmanuel Levinas shortly, but we already understand that these are essential keys to taking into account, for example, happiness itself at work, human beings, the environment, and so on.

A crucial question is whether – instead of the wider application of the dominant economic paradigm we have described – one couldn't instead talk about what Louis van Bladel (1993, 519) already a quarter of a century ago called an explicitly *ethical extension* of the economy. In this, rational analysis becomes a necessary (but not sufficient) precondition for a reasonable choice. De Dijn also states explicitly that a plea for reasonableness does not imply denial of the concept of instrumental rationality as important in specifically restricted ("technical") areas (Parret, 131). So we're not advocating a mere replacement of instrumental rationality by ethical reason, or the slavish subordination of reason to economic rationality, or the unscrupulous separation of both. With Luk Bouckaert, we advocate an *ethical economy*, thus a kind of *reasonable rationality* (Boey, 1993, 287). Hereby, the separation between economy and ethics – as it has been posited since the very beginning of economic science – is transcended. In a similar spirit, we aspire in this book to transcend the opposition between dystopia and utopia.

Ethical Economy

What was the relationship between the economy and ethics before ethical reason was conquered by instrumental rationality at the beginning of modernity? If we hope to found the ethical economy well, with an eye to transcending the tension between dystopia and utopia, it seems more than fair to substantiate our answer. We've seen that, from the emergence of economic science at the end of the eighteenth century, there was one current that considered the economy separate from ethics, and another that kept these two together. As this "keeping together" still amounted to a clear supremacy of rationality, we want to investigate whether any visions had been developed – before the emergence of economic science – in which the economy was in relationship with ethics, without ethics being used and abused by the economy.

Embedding

In this search, we consult Marcel Becker,[65] who refers to the period from Antiquity to the Middle Ages. During that period, one might speak of something operating that Becker calls a *relationship of embedding* between economics and ethics (Becker, 2001, 39), although as far back as Socrates the economy was in service to, but also in

[65] This chapter is based on Chapter 1 of Becker (2001). See also Sedláček (2011).

harmony with, the good life in which human happiness is realized. Aristotle draws on this idea to emphasize the importance of justice. He also demonstrates how economic activities that he called *necessary* activities, or *ascholia* (Greek for "*work; earning a living; not at leisure*"), acted as a means to an end, this end being the *essential* activity, or *scholê* (Greek for "*the pursuit of an expanding use of time to develop the mind, body, and spirit*"). This subservience *and* harmony also appear in his description of economics as a domestic science, whereby the steward takes upon himself the management of the goods in the service of the general interest. "Economics was not an autonomous discipline, but embedded in (that is, subservient to and steered by) the larger whole of a philosophical and ethical orientation toward a good life for the people of the community" (Becker, 2001, 41). Today, we may posit that this subservience was transformed into autonomy and leads to a dystopia that is damaging the good life.

In the Middle Ages, the subservient "embedment relationship" between economics and ethics was taken over in the philosophy of Thomas Aquinas, among others. Here is a concrete example of his view of money (which we'll see being transformed into the philosophy of Emmanuel Levinas in Chapter 6): If you want money to provide happiness in a reasonable way, you must take the nature of the money into account. It is the natural function of money to exchange services and goods, not to earn *extra* money. You could possibly give it away, or you could buy a book with it. But if you put banknotes you would normally use to buy the book on the windowsill in the sun, it will not grow extra money. That is not how things work. This unnatural state of affairs occurs when, through interest, you demand more money back, more than you initially gave, for the money you lent (Becker, 42).

At the transition from the Middle Ages to modernity, we see the last attempts to sustain this prohibition on interest. One of the central characters in this endeavour is Thomas Aquinas's fifteenth-century fellow Dominican, Girolamo Savonarola (Sebregondi, 2011). He railed against the manipulations of interest that resulted in the emergence and grand display of wealth by the rich. In 1497, Savonarola went so far as to have several paintings that showed off wealth burned at the Piazza della Signoria in Florence. Even the well-known painter Sandro Botticelli, who had become deeply devout under Savonarola's influence, contributed some of his splashier, more flamboyant works on pagan themes to the fire. Is it not true today, as well, that we are confronted with a growing inequality of income, with luxury trends such as hyped-up cruises, refurbished luxury hotels and the search for consolation in all kinds of wellness products and services? Savonarola, however, did not merely question the flamboyant display of wealth. More fundamental was his finger-wagging at the Medici family, for allowing Jewish bank institutions to demand exorbitant interest rates. Up until the time of the Medici policy, Christian banks had done as much as possible to respect ethics, just as Islamic banks today handle the question of interest carefully. But we also see initiatives to implement ethical banking in many different places today, in Europe (EthikBank, Hefboom, Triodos), North America (Urban Partnership, First Green, New Resource) and Oceania (Bankmecu, Prometheu) – just some of the banks that are linking ethical criteria to their investments. As we've established, money cannot just spontaneously generate money.

Separation

At the beginning of this chapter, we described the attempts to avoid a separation between ethics and economics that emerged at the dawn of economic science. In spite of this, we saw that the immoral character of the economy eventually prevailed over amorality, and certainly over morality. An amoral economy, for example, leaves open the question of whether money makes us happy or not. The immoral character of the economy becomes obvious at the moment this economy turns into a dystopia (think of the growing income inequality). Becker argues that the demise of a normative framework for the economy implies an egotistical individual who is thrown back on himself, a person who presents unlimited needs and asocial behaviours. "Moreover, an economy of endless growth would activate the destruction of man and the environment" (Becker, 42).

Becker links the actual separation of ethics and economics to two kinds of ethics that emerged with modernity: deontology (to fulfil one's obligations) and utilitarianism (to optimize one's usefulness). Kant's deontology might very well provide a framework to preserve human dignity, for example; think of personnel management, whereby an employer has specific obligations. In fact, however, deontology doesn't square with an economy in which human beings and material goods are viewed as exchange values, and certainly not as values that entail specific obligations. That means that deontology can at best fiddle somewhat in the margins. Utilitarianism, or the theory of usefulness, conquered the heart of the economy. Think of the end of the Middle Ages, when they definitively opted for the raising of, or shall we call it *practising*, usury with interest rates. The founder of utilitarianism, Jeremy Bentham (1787), purposely called his bible of utilitarianism "*Defense of Usury*". As we'll see in Chapter 5, the association of economics with the theory of usefulness resulted in the fact that, from that moment forward, global human happiness was subjugated to the narrow Gross National Product at the expense of larger concepts such as Gross National Happiness.

Dialogue

When, as with Aristotle, ethics revert to the ethics of virtues, we enter a dialogue between *rational* (deontological or utilitarian) and *reasonable* starting points for economic practice. A virtue is a positive quality someone possesses in view of correct behaviour. By once again giving the virtue of *justice* a central place in the *economy*, in the following chapters, we will be able to search for a framework in which happiness holds prominence, for the individual as well as for society.

The development of frameworks by thinkers like Martha Nussbaum – who just happens to have written her doctoral dissertation on Aristotle – further enables us to connect with already mentioned moral experiences or emotions, such as fear, suffering, hope and longing. Those experiences allowed us to explore the economy both as dystopia and as utopia. At first sight, Nussbaum's integration of moral experiences, specifically emotions, corresponds with the attention Stoics gave them in the past. Actually, emotions are reasonable pronouncements that value something. They imbue things we do not control rationally with importance. Something has value because it moves us. However, Nussbaum does not come to the Stoics' conclusion, that emotions are bad counsellors for humans and society. In her opinion, on the contrary, they constitute the foundations of ethical life (2001). They put us on the road to a specific knowledge, and are viewed as intelligent or cognitive processes. True, the information they provide is processed in a non-rational way to a large extent, but it is not therefore also less relevant. On the contrary.

Nussbaum here concurs with the present trend in psychological and neuroscientific research concerning emotions. Emotions provide us with information about (what we deem important in) reality. Far from negligible and dismissible, they are essential as the foundation of, in Aristotle's words, a life that is or is not fulfilled and happy (*eudaimonia*). Here we recognize what we alluded to before: an emotion such as hope can be the foundation of utopian ethical behaviour. The hope for a better society can stimulate you to make concrete changes. An emotion such as fear runs the risk of becoming the foundation of dystopian ethical behaviour. Fear of the permanent shortage of anything and everything (from bread to luxury cruises) made our economy blow its fuses. Behaviour is no longer founded, as with Kant, upon knowledge through exclusively rational insight. Our moral behaviour may just as well be founded upon knowledge that is based upon our reasonable empathy for our own feelings (such as fear) as upon concern for the feelings of others (sympathy). In the latter case, our behaviour amounts to compassion, something we'll explore in detail shortly. As was posited by Socrates, we retain the philosophical starting point that knowledge is the foundation of our behaviour. But we increasingly realize that the non-rational (such as emotions) can provide us with knowledge that is just as relevant.

Compassion as Meaningfulness in the Economy

As early as 1759, in his *Theory of Moral Sentiments*, the economist and philosopher of ethics Adam Smith argued that moral behaviour stems from a feeling of empathy, the ability to place oneself in someone else's feelings or thoughts. Nussbaum bases herself on this when – addressing the educational process – she stresses the importance of literature in order to strengthen feelings of empathy. Empathy can lead to compassion. In English, one speaks of *compassion* or *mercy*. They are often synonyms, except in the distinction between "compassion" as *sympathy* and "mercy" as *grace*. By "mercy", we understand something greater than sympathy. Sympathy is a feeling of sorrow for someone else that can happen to you outside of your control. Compassion involves a concrete attitude towards the other, a feeling that can be stimulated by sympathy, among other things, but one that we also can choose knowingly. In Chapter 5, compassion will become crucial in an economy that is not merely based upon the emotion of fear.

It's not for nothing that the notion of *Gross National Happiness* that we've described emerged in a country like Bhutan, where Buddhism accords a central place to compassion for one's fellow man and with nature. In Christianity (and in Islam as well[66]) compassion is called mercy. In the parable of the Good Samaritan (Luke, 10: 25–37), we witness a summary of this, which is also an appeal that was already present among earlier Jewish prophets. The Good Samaritan was moved by sympathy and did everything he could to help the man who had been mugged. In Judaism, mercy is actually much more linked to duty, whereas in Christianity it is based upon the goodness of and trust in God (Illich, 2014). Pope Francis declared 2016 to be the *Year of Mercy*, not only with regard to interpersonal relations, but also in economic, social and ecological domains. Similarly, the Good Samaritan doesn't just honour a personal commitment, but seems to set up something like the beginning of a social-security system: "The next morning he produced two silver pieces and gave them to the innkeeper, and said: 'Look after him; and if you spend any more, I will repay you on my way back'" (Luke, 10, 35). We will return to this transition from the personal to the institutional in Chapter 4, with Paul Ricœur.

The amazing thing is that between 800 and 200 BCE – in the West, with Socrates, as well as in the East with Confucius in China and the Buddha in India, but also in the Middle East with the Prophet Jeremiah – compassion takes a front-row seat. According to the philosopher Karl Jaspers, that period of history is crucial, for it was a period in which those societies were confronted with many dystopian elements, just like today. These challenges gave rise to new attitudes, such as compassion. Jaspers talks here about an *Achsenzeit*, in English an "*Axial*", *or pivotal, age*. The emphasis on compassion since the Axial

[66] In Islam, *The Most Merciful* (*Ar-Rahman*) is one of the most frequent names for God. Especially during Ramadan, faithful Muslims are not only called to fast and pray, but also to exercise mercy, for example by giving alms.

Age was furthermore accompanied by the insight that every human being in society is as valuable as any other. With that, the great inequality in society appeared in the cross-hairs.

Equality and Democracy

Through compassion, we also rediscover the importance of more equality in our society. Compassion starts from the desirability of more equality and acts accordingly. According to Nussbaum, *eudaimonia* – or the blossoming and happy existence of man and environment – can only be assured through sufficient (democratic) equality. This happens concretely by taking all potential human capacities (the *capability approach* in economics) into account. In this process, rational as well as reasonable (relational, creative and emotional) elements are involved. A happy life doesn't just ensure material goods such as food, drink and protection, but non-material goods such as culture, friendship and love, in at least equal measure.

At the end of Chapter 5, we'll see how, in Bhutan, these diverse facets are central when it comes to measuring what they call Gross National Happiness. An economy that is geared too much to rationally or materially oriented human capacities leads to the obsession with increasing Gross National Product, with its potential dystopian effects. When, on the other hand, you pay too much attention to non-rational or non-material aspects, you end up in the other extreme, an abstract utopia. That is why we tend to advocate what Ernst Bloch calls *a concrete utopia*. A concrete utopia entails a vision that can indeed be attained, whereas an abstract utopia expresses an unworldly fantasy. That is why the breakthrough of democracy is important in Bhutan, as we shall see further on.

In the foreword to *De mythe van de groene economie* ("*The Myth of the Green Economy*"), Erik Swyngedouw wonders what we are lacking in confronting dystopia, or, as he puts it (Kenis, 2012, 23), "to *really* tackle the socio-ecological apocalypse [my italics]". As he puts it, the fundamental problem consists of the fact that we do not take seriously the foundation of our democratic society, to wit democratic equality, as an ethical starting point: "Democratic equality is not a sociologically verifiable reality – we all know that every concrete society contains many inequalities that are clearly observable – but an axiomatic principle. So democracy means precisely that we start from the assumption that all people are equal." To ensure that this doesn't remain utopian, he advocates "the conversion of the egalitarian demand to concrete socio-ecological equality". According to Swyngedouw, this requires "intellectual courage", "social mobilization" and "action and organization". In the present book, we'll also arrive at this need for courage, mobilization and action. But complementary to this vision, we're talking about courage, mobilization and action as they express themselves interpersonally and structurally through compassion. Just as democracy starts from the conviction that all people are equal, compassion too views all people as equal.

In Chapter 6, with Levinas, we'll see that *equality* comes down to *equivalence*. One might say that equivalence transcends the traditional opposition between equality and inequality. Men and women are not equal in the sense that they are *identical*, but in the spirit of the principle of equality, they are definitely *equivalent*. Just as one can only muster compassion when one sets out from the conviction that people are not unequal, the alternative to what Swyngedouw calls "the scandal of institutionalized democracy" (Kenis, 2016, 23) can only take shape when you begin with the assumption that people are equivalent. This shaping of the nuanced concept of equivalence in an economic context might help us better understand not just how brutal equality resulted in communism, but also how Alexis de Tocqueville describes the hypothetical equality of all people as the foundation of the capitalism that he sees emerging in the USA in 1847, and eventually resulting in the inequality of the people. Certainly, in the present period of populist recipes, the concept of equivalence is crucially important. It casts a different light on the seemingly insoluble tension between the left (which loathes the rich) and the right (which neglects immigrants).

Swyngedouw's foreword ends with the following sentence: "We have nothing to lose but our fear" (Kenis, 2016, 23). As we learned in the previous chapter, trust as the foundation for compassion comes down to abandoning our fear. However, in order to grasp the very early emergence of our present-day dystopian economy, it appears to be rather important not to focus exclusively on positive feelings such as empathy and compassion. That is why, in the wake of philosophers of contract such as Hobbes, we also have to take negative feelings, such as fear, suffering and envy, into account. After a short while, the tension between equality and inequality will surface again here as well, but without the notion of equivalence that is linked to authentic compassion and real democracy.

4. Philosophers of Contract and the Paradoxical Context of the Economy

With Hans Achterhuis in Mind

The opposition between economic dystopia and utopia doesn't just reflect the relationship between fear and desire, economics and ethics, rationality and reasonableness. It appears that it is also closely linked to the starting point of the economy, to wit, scarcity. The economy searches for a way to abolish scarcity as efficiently as possible. In his standard work, *Het Rijk van de Schaarste* ("*The Realm of Scarcity*"), the inspiration for this chapter, Hans Achterhuis (1988) asserts that scarcity is a central notion in economics. When combating scarcity, you risk quickly ending up in dystopian or utopian realms. One could easily point out the negative but simultaneously attractive effects of both a communist and a capitalist economy, both of which aim to combat scarcity.

It is important to note that Achterhuis links scarcity to emotions such as fear and desire. Thus, in the theories of the seventeenth-century philosopher Thomas Hobbes, Achterhuis discovers the origins of the permanent creation of scarcity. In his book *Leviathan* (1651), Hobbes indeed encounters the phenomenon of fear: "*Fear and I were twins.*" Up until today, philosophers have pointed at fear as the foundation of society. Think of Jean-Paul Sartre's statement "*Nous sommes peur*" ("*We are fear*"). And of Martha Nussbaum, who starts her essay in the recently published *The World Book of Hope* with the phenomenon of fear (Bormans, 2016).

This is why we'll first explore the way philosophers of contract – such as Hobbes and Locke – look at fear, as well as desire. Philosophers of contract develop a social agreement, a contract, in which the state, thanks to the approval of the citizens, endeavours to keep a balance between dystopia and utopia. This is a new perspective, whether it happens in a democratic way or not, because it is no longer based on the approval of a god. The agreement you conclude means that you are switching over from a natural to a social context. Thanks to the state, economic development can take place, for without a state, the economy degenerates into violence. In Chapter 5, where philosophers of responsibility will replace the philosophers of contract, it will become obvious that the emphasis will be laid on citizens. As a result of the limitations of the state, the responsibility to transcend the tension between dystopia and utopia falls to citizens. Today, this democratic character has become all the more important. We'll see that an economy without responsible citizens leads to new forms of violence.

The Necessity of a Just Contract

Movement as the natural foundation of the economy

As a philosopher of contract, Hobbes consciously distances himself from the reasonableness that had dominated medieval philosophy from antiquity right up until his time at Oxford. Achterhuis (1988, 19) explains how Hobbes, during his regular trips to Italy, was totally fascinated by the rational scientific methods of Galileo Galilei and others. For Galileo, a central concept is that of *movement*. In *Leviathan*, Hobbes strives to extend the concept of movement to the study of the economy and society. Even today, we recognize the economy's permanent state of being in motion in some of the characteristics that we have called economic dystopia: money has to be moving constantly (even when the financial system is running smoothly); the economy (Gross National Product) has to grow continuously (even when this ruins the environment); he who comes to an economic standstill is a loser (despite the risk of a burnout when one never stands still) … Thus, the advocacy of sustainable growth in order to optimize happiness (Gross National Happiness) is a way of questioning the primacy of movement. For Hobbes, however, human happiness is not determined by the peace of a satisfied mind, for he views happiness as never-ending movement, a perpetual progress of desire.

Furthermore, according to Hobbes, the most typical expression of man is the expression of a specific movement, namely threatening the other. The natural state of man is that of a threefold movement of threat: People "attack one another … to *achieve profits*, to *live in safety* … and to *maintain a high reputation* [my emphasis]" (1988, 21). What were human vices before modernity have here turned into objective human characteristics. According to Hobbes, human beings are not what they were for Aristotle, who called them social and political beings. They're envious individuals to whom the other constitutes a threat. Ricœur, who died at the onset of the twenty-first century, stressed the importance of the core human impulses behind Hobbes' threefold movement of man: *avoir* (to have, to possess), *pouvoir* (to be able to) and *valoir* (to assert oneself). Only by linking well-balanced institutions (respectively, the economy, politics and culture) to these three human drivers can we prevent, according to Ricœur, the victory of evil, that is, of dystopia. In Hobbes' world, people threaten one another not only as individuals, but also as states.

Power and equality

Hobbes saw it as typical of humans that individual and social threats are based on distrust, the opposite of trust. Earlier, we encountered the importance of trust as the foundation upon which we may proceed from fear and suffering to happiness. Actually, the tension between movement and standstill (also recognizable in the relationship between distrust and trust) has been with us since antiquity. Heraclitus and other pre-Socratic thinkers in what is now Turkey had already stressed the fact that everything is constantly changing, while Parmenides and other pre-Socratics who lived in what is now southern Italy argued that, in the end, nothing changes. Aristotle spoke of rest as our natural state. Hobbes, however, followed Heraclitus' vision that war (for Hobbes: *movement*) is the father of everything. Even the longing for peace and quiet is a kind of movement.

For Hobbes, the omnipresent individual and societal movements boil down to a struggle for power. Thus, an institution such as the economy is – or isn't – a good product of an imperative "struggle for power". In line with what Ricœur sees in institutions, Hobbes posits: "Wealth, knowledge, and honor are different forms of power" (1988, 23). The Latin word *competere* (literally, *to befit*), from which *competition* (read: power struggle) is derived, first and foremost means "to try to achieve one point together", which illustrates that economic power does not have to be formulated in the negative per se. On the contrary.

According to Hobbes, however, power as the foundation of a power struggle meant that men wish to differentiate themselves from other men, on the basis of their (physical, mental, financial, etc.) abilities. So it looks as if money brings us happiness, in so far as we can use this money and the goods we purchase with it to trump our fellow human beings. In *Leviathan*, Hobbes summarizes this as follows: "The competition for riches, honor, authority, and other kinds of power leads to quarrels, enmity and war. For a competitor can only obtain that which he desires by killing, subjecting, surpassing, or chasing away the other" (1988, 24).

To understand the power struggle in Hobbes' terms correctly, it is crucial to remember that he assumes that all people dispose of quasi-equal abilities to distinguish themselves from other people. It is this equality of all people that leads to a general power struggle in society. For if it is true – as we'll see later, with the philosopher of culture René Girard, who died at the end of 2015 – that people are constantly able to desire what others desire (mimetic desire), then all goods will become scarce eventually. It is striking how strongly Hobbes emphasizes this so-called natural equality of all human beings. Actually, he views this equality between human beings as just as natural as the natural hierarchy that Aristotle talked about, or as the caste system that we still encounter today in a country such as India. Something about the "natural state" of this equality, as Hobbes saw this, still surfaces today in terms such as "*handicapped persons*". In society, we assume that people dispose of a comparable degree of physical and mental abilities, and when this is not the case, we talk of "*people with a physical or mental handicap*" – sort of the exceptions that confirm the rule of equality. Hobbes posits very clearly that, even if nature hadn't made people equal, we have to assume this by way of an additional agreement, or natural law, that establishes that everyone has to acknowledge everyone else as his natural equal. Everybody wants bread, energy, water, land, etc. When, however, as a result of the power struggle, a society threatens to collapse into conflict or war (whether it is the struggle for oil or, more recently, for water), human (read: economic) coexistence becomes impossible. Hobbes talks of "a war of all against all" (1988, 25–32).

Fear and desire in justly observed laws

As we indicated, Hobbes emphasizes the importance of emotions such as fear and desire. He talks about the importance of the fear of death and the desire (or hope) for happiness. It is clear to Hobbes that a society can only survive when man links his rational tendency to gain movement to emotions such as fear and longing in a reasonable way. Here we see a clear illustration of what we called the need for a reasonable rationality. A system built on such a reasonable rationality can only survive when one sticks to specific agreements, which Hobbes also called the conditions for peace, or natural laws. Let us take a closer look at these natural laws of Hobbes. Achterhuis rightly argues that the first two are the most important ones.

Hobbes' first law of nature entails that, "in order to escape the war of all against all, in which their lives are constantly threatened, people must search and strive for peace" (1988, 26). As this first law of nature goes, the fact that we feel threatened, the emotion of fear, lies at the origin, whereby the focus is on the subject, the I, who is afraid. The second law of nature entails that "someone, if and when others agree to the same, must be prepared to relinquish his right to all things, in as far as he deems this necessary for peace or in his own defense, and to be satisfied with as much freedom for others as he would have others award to him" (1988, 26). Here the emotion of hope for happiness – for myself and for the Other – comes first. We recognize in this a specific expression of what one calls the Golden Rule, or what boils down to Kant's categorical imperative: *Act only according to that maxim whereby you can at the same time will that it should become a universal law.*

To make these two fundamental rules of life work for a successful (economic) coexistence, Hobbes argues they must be secured in an agreement, or contract, of coexistence. As with Aristotle, justice occupies a central place here, and it will consist of honouring the agreements that result from such a contract. Once again, it is interesting to engage with Ricœur here. In the seventh chapter of his book *Soi-même comme un autre* (*Oneself as Another*) (1990), he explains how the *subject* (the first law of nature) can only coexist with the other (the second law of nature) when an institution guarantees this in a contract (i.e. the theory of contract). According to Hobbes, this is the way the state comes into being. In the social contract, people transfer their natural rights to the state.

For Hobbes, to avoid civil war, it is important to ensure that the rights of those who govern the state be absolute. This is how an absolute ruler with undivided sovereignty emerges. However, the fear of death and the desire for a happy life – the two laws of nature – also form the basis for a responsible escape from the sovereignty of the ruler (1988, 28). We can see a translation of this idea that self-preservation (really, the interests of the citizen) should prevail over the interests of the state in modern Bhutan, where the king, as the inspiration of an economy of happiness, is gradually allowing the development of democracy.

Transcending the ego

It is important to understand that merely the fear of suffering (first law of nature) isn't sufficient as an incentive for the ethical economy we're looking for. To avoid ending up in a dystopia of fear, one ought, in the spirit of the second law of nature, to develop a reasonable form of economic compassion alongside an often-unavoidable rational competitive economic war. This, instead of resigning ourselves to an individualistic dystopian economy, or one that is based on fear, or limiting ourselves to act purely out of mutual interest. At the end of Chapter 3, we referred already to the importance of compassion. On the basis of his comparative philosophy, the Belgian philosopher Ulrich Libbrecht (1928–2017) indicates (2014) that it is one-sided to limit oneself to one's ego-intentionality. In this, everyone eventually defends himself and happiness is strongly linked to the ego. The application of compassion towards all living beings, including nature, imposes itself.[67] Here, Libbrecht refers to the Gross National Happiness of Bhutan: "For what is then the goal of the economy? Certainly not the enrichment of a few, but the happiness of all. Today, Bhutan is perhaps the last purely Buddhist country that is nevertheless carefully venturing on the path to modernization. In that country, the goal is not the Gross National Product, but the Gross National Happiness … Economy appropriates, love shares, and, as love extends to all living

[67] In this sense, Libbrecht talks of an economy "that is no longer driven by egoism, but by the love of one's neighbor, with as a main goal not personal enrichment, but the fight against poverty and inequality" (2014, 115).

beings, the protection of nature is of the utmost importance" (2014, 74). We are immediately reminded of the thesis of De Grauwe, that the environment is the Achilles heel of a more ethical economy. Along the lines of Hobbes' *Fear and I were born twins together*, Libbrecht views emotionality primarily as ego-intentional. However, when one is emotionally moved (by the mystery of nature, for example), "higher" feelings that transcend the ego can arise. "There also exist emotions that are directed toward the Mystery, that are thus transcendent in the sense that they transcend immanent emotions" (2014, 52). We conclude that emotions such as fear and suffering are at the source of our desire to satisfy the purely material needs of the ego. Higher emotions, such as longing and hope, however, can appeal to our compassion for other living beings.

The Paradox of Scarcity

At this point, it is important to examine, together with Achterhuis, the insights about the origin of scarcity that another philosopher of contract, John Locke, developed in the seventeenth century, almost half a century after Hobbes. With Locke (*Two Treatises on Government*, 1689), we encounter an interesting philosopher, as he doesn't approach the question of meaningfulness (in the economy) in a polarizing way, but on the contrary assumes that we can only survive as a society when we remain receptive to other opinions. For Locke, a Christian of serious conviction, it is wrong to posit that one religion would be better than the other. Or, as one heard on occasion of the *Year of Mercy* in 2016, that "Christian mercy is more radical than Buddhist compassion". In terms of our concrete commitment to fellow human beings and to nature, in Christianity as well as in Buddhism, you will find factions that are more radical than others. In an actively pluralistic way, Locke is open to diverse points of view, something he translated politically in his plea for democracy. In the economy, he did this with his plea for a free market that enables the development of a diversity of enterprises.

Locke links the origin of scarcity explicitly to the introduction of money. He assumes that, in the state of nature, there wasn't any scarcity. In any event, there was enough land for everybody. Compare this to Bhutan today, where everyone is guaranteed a piece of land, and where the king even releases some of his own land when citizens find themselves without. Locke posited that the introduction of money put an end to the natural state in which there was no problem of scarcity. When people start to own money (and we're not even talking about excessive speculation), they begin to desire more than they can effectively spend, with all this entails for economic growth and its impact. Here Achterhuis quotes Locke, from paragraph 49 of *Two Treatises on Government:* "Find out something that hath the use and value of money among his neighbours, you shall see the same man [who initially was satisfied with sufficient goods for himself and his family] will begin presently to enlarge his possessions" (1988, 30). Achterhuis is right to speak of the paradox of scarcity; economy did not emanate from scarcity, but rather induced it. Thus, everything becomes scarce: welfare, health, clean water, clean air, even time and silence (1988, 13).

Mimetic Desire and Compassion

According to Locke, money plays a key role in the origins of the economy. But René Girard's concept of *mimetic desire* is even more fundamental to the origins of the economy of scarcity. Of course, philosophers such as Aristotle and Rousseau have already pointed out the importance of *mimesis*, or imitation, for man. Girard (1923–2015) refers to Aristotle, who stated that man distinguishes himself from other animals because he is better at imitating. But Girard takes it further. Humans constantly desire what others desire. With his 1988 book *Het Rijk van de Schaarste* ("*The Realm of Scarcity*"), Achterhuis was one of the first to clearly explain the impact of this new concept on the economy. Also, philosophers like Louis Van Bladel did it. Along with Achterhuis and Van Bladel (1980), but also with Paul Dumouchel (1979) who inspired Achterhuis and van Bladel, we must still stress the importance of this crucial new concept from René Girard.

Girard was describing a specific kind of imitation as the foundation of our society and economy: imitating, or mimetic desire. Here, the other person is no longer a model, but a rival. According to Girard, a conflict emerges on the basis of a continuous mimetic desire. This conflict always originates when two people desire the same thing. This can be anything from an ordinary object to a unique woman they both desire. As a result of a kind of mimetic contagion, the entire group to which both belong can come under the spell of mimetic desire. In the end, all this anger turns against one person, who is then killed as a scapegoat, with the effect that the group regains peace. Girard views this sacrifice of scapegoats as the foundation of our culture and economy. With the slaughter of the scapegoat (which is assumed to be at the origin of the chaos) restored the peace, people start to revere the scapegoat in religion.

Mimetic desire appears to be grounded in the tragic human fact of a shortage of compassion. At the same time, it is compassion that will constitute the heart of an economy (of happiness) that seeks an answer to the dystopia that is generated by scarcity. In his book *Des choses cachées depuis la fondation du monde* ("*Things Hidden Since the Foundation of the World*"), Girard refers to the primal story of Cain and Abel. In the spirit of the state of nature, Locke already said that, in the beginning, Cain could take as much land as he could cultivate, and yet leave enough for Abel to graze his flock on. Here, Girard points at the fact that Cain killed his brother Abel the moment he realized that his brother enjoyed that which he himself cherished but was utterly lacking, namely compassion. In this story, that compassion is expressed in the mercy or love of God. In this sense, it isn't money that starts the economy, money that might or might not make you happy, but the experience of compassion or love. Think also of the living, warm light of the Buddha, as the ultimate guarantee that, within Buddhism, one will eventually be released from suffering. Both Cain and Abel were offering a sacrifice to God, but it appeared that only the smoke of Cain's sacrifice was rising to God in heaven. However, we read in the Bible that God explicitly warned Cain not to compete with his brother. Envy and desire are designated as sins.

Economy as Religion

Girard reminds us once again of Hobbes' vision, according to which equality among people is important for the emergence of a competitive society and economy. According to Girard, however, growing equality between humans doesn't only result in more competition, but also in scarcity and violence. For when people are more and more equal, the person who mimics the desire of another person (first as a model, and finally as a rival) comes dangerously close to the other person: "In a world of equality, the models and rivals multiply, everything is constantly moving, stability has been lost forever" (1988, 116).

Also inspired by the philosopher Paul Dumouchel, Achterhuis summarizes the question that, in the end, remains with René Girard in a razor-sharp way: "If the mimetic conflict between people who are equal is unavoidable, how then are … culture and society possible?" (1988, 117). Or, more specifically geared to our topic: how does the economy stay afloat in spite of the dystopia it creates? The economy is sinking; long live the economy? The answer is that the economy, after it has fought economic scarcity, once again creates a scarcity, which it then has to eliminate. This actually boils down to economic growth having turned into another religion. It appears that the survival of the economy is founded on the elimination and repetitive staging, and defying, of scarcity, just as with the scapegoat, or in the Catholic Church each time that holy mass (the Eucharist) is celebrated. Time and again, economic growth is induced by eliminating scarcity, but then also by creating *new* forms of scarcity, which have to be fought anew. You might call this specific view of meaningfulness in the economy a sort of religion.

We also discern this mechanism of creating and eliminating scarcity in the victims created by the economy. As a result of this, they look like scapegoats. When, for example, more and more people are suffering from burnout owing to the pressure of economic performance, we notice that the system tries to appear healing again. It does this by inventing all kinds of attenuating measures (such as time credit and the like). These might bring some temporary relief, but they do not prevent the fact that the employees must become more productive once again. Actually, as a result, even more people are confronted with burnout. Never is the very logic of capitalism – the primacy of the continuous growth of the scarcity economy, that is, the religion of economy – fundamentally questioned. The Third World functions the same way: it is exploited, but time and again, some developmental help is then offered. Closer to home, you might think of the plight of the Fourth World (the poor among us) that is never really healed, while at the same time we keep organizing actions against poverty. Think of Mark Zuckerberg, of Facebook, who donates a large part of his income. In the end, nature (or the climate) appears to be the ultimate victim of the economy of scarcity. Which was also the insight of Paul de Grauwe in the first chapter. But just as well, the neoliberal economy he describes attempts to protect the environment, time and again. From one climate conference to the next, nature, in its quasi-scapegoat function, is celebrated as in high mass. We are demonstrating and singing for the climate. Doing all this, we never really question capitalism itself. On the contrary: investments in climate technologies give a distressed capitalism a fresh boost, just as war technologies do.

Strictly speaking, the employees with their burnout, the Third and Fourth Worlds and the polluted environment are thus victims of our economy. In each case, we're talking about someone or something that is hit by the consequences of our economic acts or events. However, the guilt is always laid upon a scapegoat. Figuratively speaking, the victims we just mentioned are scapegoats of the economic system. That is to say, whoever or whatever is systematically the object of harassment. This is certainly the case with the average employee in our economic system. The same goes for the Third and Fourth Worlds, and the environment. Each time, they're subjected to harassment, not to mention abused. But even when we use the term "scapegoat" literally as in "whoever or whatever is blamed", we can see that this is also the case with the employee who has come under pressure. One will say that the employee who is costing us too much must be the cause of our loss of competitiveness. Also, the poor from the Third or Fourth World are blamed as being too lazy to work their way up. Last but not least, the fundamental Western attitude towards nature entails the latter being more a threat than a treasure for man. So we are not guilty; nature itself is. Which, of course, doesn't square with respect for its biodiversity. Just as with the mechanism of the scapegoat, instead of looking for the real causes of the problems, we hold someone or something innocent responsible. We see confirmation of these theses in the work of Achterhuis, who explains how third parties are constantly the victims of the fight against scarcity: "The third parties are not scapegoats in the traditional view. They are much more numerous than the scapegoats ever were. They are, however, sacrificed as scapegoats. This time, not in order to overcome incidental scarcity, but precisely to keep the eternal crisis of modern scarcity afloat" (1988, 217).

The Paradox of Christianity

Let us accompany Achterhuis and Dumouchel a little further in the search for the roots of the economy of scarcity and dystopia. A negative, but time and again soothing attitude towards the victims created by the economy of scarcity has indeed elevated this economy to a new religion in our society. But how could the struggle of the economy against scarcity have replaced the scapegoat rituals of traditional religion and installed a desacralized society? To resolve this question, if we wish to combat economic dystopia, we'll have to focus our analysis on the crucial forms of responsibility that are presenting themselves. We're talking here of compassion and solidarity. At the end of Chapter 3, we defined compassion as a concretely consistent attitude towards the other, for whom you consciously choose, whether or not moved by sympathy. Solidarity deals rather with *togetherness*, the consequences of which you are prepared to accept. With solidarity, rationality is predominant, while with compassion, one is more confronted with reasonableness in terms of the unconditional. That is, with solidarity and compassion, we get a glimpse of more efficient solutions for the victims that the economy has created, than we do with a repeatedly soothing attitude towards them.

Along the lines of René Girard, Paul Dumouchel formulates this as follows: "Scarcity is the result of the demise of the obligations to solidarity which united the community. It is the systematic transgression of the traditional prohibitions. It is the conscious refusal of the anti-mimetic protection that was offered by the sacred and by religion. This reversal regarding the sacred and religion creates, as a social construction, a totality of goods and resources which is such that the needs and desires of all people can no longer be satisfied" (1988, 53). In other words, turning away from the sacred creates an economy of scarcity as a dystopia, which becomes visible through victims such as the employee who burns out on the job, the poor in the Third and Fourth Worlds, and, last but not least, the environment and the climate.

It would take us too far afield to sketch, in this essay, the decisive role that the Judaeo-Christian tradition played in the emergence of capitalism – more specifically, as this manifested itself in Protestantism's encouragement of thrift, which made the breakthrough concept of investments possible, which in turn helped give rise to capitalism (Tawney, 1938). It is, however, striking how in the course of the ensuing development of capitalism, this Judaeo-Christian tradition simultaneously allowed its exegetes to demolish the religious efficiency of the scapegoat phenomenon. Jesus of Nazareth did not have to be killed as a guilty scapegoat in order to save us from (the consequences of) our persistent mimetic desire. We ourselves elicit violence towards the victims over and over. The fact that we keep repeating the sacrificing of Jesus of Nazareth (as still is the case in the Catholic celebration of the Eucharist) is to no avail in this matter. This form of sacrament has been unmasked by the Judaeo-Christian tradition. We find a telling illustration of this unmasking in the following passage from the beginning of Bach's masterpiece the *St Matthew Passion*. Is this the reason why people still find consolation in this musical masterpiece today (Opdebeeck, 2017)? With Bach (1685–1750), we are at the high point of the Enlightenment, a time when industrialization was able to break through by means of science and technology:

O Lamm Gottes unschuldig
Am Stamm des Kreuzes geschlachtet,
Allzeit erfund'n geduldig,
Wiewohl du warest verachtet.

O innocent Lamb of God
Slaughtered on the cross,
Always patient,
Though thou wast despised.

So one may speak of the paradox of the Judaeo-Christian role in the economy of scarcity. On the one hand, it stimulated the emergence of that economy as a new religion. On the other, it deprived the economy of the chance to point at religion as a chance to forgive our debts through the expiatory sacrifice of Christ. Or: to be exonerated from the violence we inflict upon our economic victims, such as the poor and nature. The evolution of Judaeo-Christian exegesis proves abundantly that we ourselves are responsible for this, that we ourselves ought to muster solidarity and compassion. As the twentieth-century philosopher and theologian Paul Tillich (1957) puts it, it is *responsible* man who is obliged to offer answers to the fundamental questions of his era. We may thus describe *responsibility* as the obligation to offer answers to the questions that confront you, and to take ownership for addressing them.

One of the most poignant aspects of this paradox is that, at the beginning of this twenty-first century, it is fundamentalist Islam that reminds us of religion's original role as a rectifying force. Islam did not experience a process of religious unmasking such as happened in Christianity, but, given the decadence that results from it, it denounces the forced economic growth of capitalism. Just before the mass exodus to Europe in 2015, the ISIS journal warned potential refugees against the sin they were about to commit by moving to the decadent, capitalist West.[68]

Since the disappearance of sacred religious commandments and prohibitions, our secularized, or desacralized, society is still struggling to muster sufficient solidarity with the victims it has itself created. In *The Rivers North of the Future* (2005), Ivan Illich explains how Christianity did indeed turn individual solidarity into institutions, but how these institutions gradually diminished or became counterproductive. Given how dramatically this affects the poor in the Third and Fourth Worlds (think, for example, of the current refugee crisis) – for as the Gospel said, "the poor you will always have with you" – another crisis, the ultimate crisis (to wit, that of climate change), clearly indicates that we cannot delay drastic measures of solidarity, especially with regard to the environment. That is, if we want to survive or, let's say, avoid Girard's catastrophe.

Fortunately, a non-religious philosophy such as Buddhism dovetails with the necessary responsibility that man must assume, whether or not it is connected to a deity. When Tillich talks about responsibility as an *obligation* (burden) to answer the great challenges of our time, we may also talk about the *enlightenment* (insight) of the Buddhist. The warm, loving light in the Great Vehicle stimulates him to demonstrate

68 See, for example, the French philosopher Michel Onfray (2016), who evolved from Islam-basher to a virtual idol of ISIS.

compassion. Hence, we realize once again that it will be interesting further on to let ourselves be inspired by this tradition.

Freedom

However, in order to reintroduce the logic of the economy in a setting of solidarity and compassion, we run the risk that when our plea dovetails too perfectly with Buddhist philosophy, it will become all too artificial, and hardly attainable. That is why, starting from an insight from Achterhuis (1988) about our third and last philosopher of contract, Jean-Jacques Rousseau, we should check whether we can't find the emerging transition (to responsibility in solidarity and compassion) just as well by starting from our own Western philosophy of Enlightenment.

Rousseau depicts man in his natural state, as someone we would call today a kind of "Buddha/Nature Man". For he is not afraid of death – in contrast to Hobbes' fear. Certainly, suffering and our internal relationship to suffering take central stage, given our natural tendency to survive. According to Rousseau, the fact that he wants to survive does not prevent natural man from also showing compassion at the same time. Rousseau also observes a balance in natural man, between his needs and the way he is able to actually fulfil these needs. There is thus no question yet of mimetic desire in the terms of Hobbes, Locke and Girard that could upset this balance, let alone any question that we could talk of scarcity. Once more, Rousseau, as if he were familiar with Buddhism (and the Gross National Happiness that resulted from it) literally claims "someone whose capacities are perfectly proportional to his desires would be perfectly happy" (1988, 125). It's not just the striking parallel with Buddhism that is remarkable here. You could also compare this to the ideas of Epicurus, Diogenes and Socrates. What's more, the similarity with the much less known but interesting *internal jihad* in Islam comes to mind. In contradistinction to the external or holy jihad, the internal jihad stresses the struggle against seductions and the ego. This is accomplished through fasting, prayer and the giving of alms.

Rousseau points to the introduction of private property as the ultimate cause of the emergence of violence and scarcity: "On the one hand, competition and rivalry, on the other hand, opposing interests, and always the desire to profit at the expense of the other; all these ills are the first result of (private) property, inseparably accompanied by the growing inequality" (1988, 127). It is remarkable that, in addition to social inequality, Rousseau also perceives the emergence of a kind of inequality *within* man. Just as the Buddha nature must deal with its ego, within the human subject, according to Rousseau, *being* and *appearance* start diverging. As a result, mimetic desire surfaces, with all the consequences thereof. Rousseau keenly points out that the construction of a kind of superstate, as was the case with his predecessor, Hobbes, doesn't provide an adequate answer to this. We could draw a parallel with the ever-threatening failure of the climate negotiations. Even the United Nations has been failing to provide definitive answers to the dystopia of the climate crisis. On the contrary, according to Rousseau, at first sight states and laws only succeed in reinforcing inequalities. Thus, in his way, he observes the emergence of economic victims, to whom we can now add the Third World and the environment. For it is evident, he says, that states and laws "did forever nail down the law of property and inequality, turned a clever appropriation into an irrevocable right, and from then onward subjected humanity to labor, slavery, and misery, in favor of a small group of ambitious people" (1988, 128). We read an echo of this in the above-mentioned foreword to *The Myth of the Green Economy* (Kenis, 2016), which describes "the scandal of institutionalized democracy".

For Rousseau, the distinction between *amour propre* and *amour de soi* is fundamental. *Amour de soi*, survival, is part of the natural order, as is the case with every living being in nature. We may think here of the *self-affirmation* that Ricœur describes in his 1990 book *Soi-même comme un autre* (*Oneself as Another*). On the other hand, *amour propre* deals with the tendency to compare oneself with other people, driven by one's emotions, and to come to the fore as a result of this. Once again, when dealing with this *amour propre*, or *love of self*, we are prompted to compare this with Buddhism: we are dealing with an expression of the ego, as a result of which people are stuck in their suffering and see their happiness slipping away. Achterhuis summarizes Rousseau's distinction between *amour de soi* and *amour propre* very effectively: "The original passions, all of which are focused on our happiness, deal with the objects they're focused on ... However, when obstacles keep the passions from the objects, then they become more concerned with the obstacles they want to remove than with their goals, and their nature changes. They become wrathful and full of hatred and the love of oneself … turns into selfish love, which is a relative feeling on which one compares with others" (1988, 141).

If you wish to combat mimetic desire, you have to expand *amour de soi.* Instead of a contract with the state (as Hobbes proposes), Rousseau says, we need a relational, or social, contract. Rousseau's *Social Contract* thus starts with the reversal of *fear*, the emotion that was at the base for Hobbes and led to the primacy of a contract with the state. For Rousseau, the foundation of his *Contract* is man, who has an essential passion for freedom and who desires to increase it, starting from his *amour de soi.* This in contrast to his pursuing his *amour propre*, or self-love, which brings him suffering out of fear, in competition with others, instead of the passion for freedom: "Man is born free, and everywhere he is in chains" (1988, 129).

Freedom vs Order

The question will be how, starting from our emotional desire for freedom, we can find further stepping-stones that will lead us to a happy society and economy instead of a dystopia based on fear. According to Rousseau, if you want to *avoid* mimetic desire, which is the result of the above-mentioned *amour propre*, there are initially two ways you can go. Just as the *personalism* we described in the Introduction transcended individualism as well as collectivism, Rousseau argues that we'll need a third way to prevent dystopia in a realistic way. The first way consists of standing as independently in life as possible. In this case, you'll try, as an individual, to give shape to your happiness independently of society, for example by choosing ascetic existence. Rousseau insists, however, that we eventually achieve nothing by severing ourselves from our human desires through asceticism. A human being remains a human being and will soon experience this asceticism as at odds with his or her freedom. Buddha also reached this insight early on his way to enlightenment. Therefore, the second way Rousseau offers is that of surrendering to society, especially collectivity. Think of nationalism or communism. Both the first and the second way Rousseau identified contain the risk of losing the freedom you so ardently desire. For you risk crashing into a wall, either of yourself (asceticism, as a purely personal performance) or of the authorities (despotism, totalitarianism and the like).

Before looking at Rousseau's third way, we should mention that it is remarkable that, in a Buddhist country such as Bhutan, one tries to avoid both ways described by Rousseau, lest one is dragged down by mimetic desire. In Bhutan they plead neither for unilateral autonomy (this might also help explain how they dare to prohibit smoking and alcohol) nor for one form or another of collectivism (democracy and the Internet are being introduced). Notwithstanding the fact that one can occasionally perceive some traits of an enlightened monarchy (think of the portraits of the king that are on display everywhere on the streets), the present king, as we indicated, has chosen to gradually pursue the path of a solidary democracy.

Starting from the tension between the two ways he described, Rousseau begins his search for a third way. The desire for a form of freedom that entails happiness drives him to search for a balance between the all too extreme freedom of the first way and the all too extreme order of the second, just as Ernst Bloch will seek, years later, in his essay *Freiheit und Ordnung, Abriß der Sozialutopien* (1986) (*Freedom and Order, Demolition of Social Utopias*). In my doctoral dissertation, I elaborated on this on the occasion of a study of the economist and ethical philosopher Ernst Friedrich Schumacher, who was inspired by Buddhism. The subtitle of my dissertation (1985) concerned "*The Difficult Synthesis of Order and Freedom*". And Achterhuis joins Bloch, saying it is "always about finding a fine-tuned balance between freedom and order" (2006, 46).[69] He correctly posits that the potential completion of the balance is bound up with the question of the contents of human nature: "Is man primordially an individual who develops himself autonomously and takes his own interests as a point of departure? Or is he, above all, a social being that can only develop as part of larger networks and institutions?"

[69] According to Meerten ter Borg (2003), as we explained in Chapter 2, the most important challenge of the economy of meaningfulness – namely what he "as an equilibrist" calls "the mix of transcendent and ontological security" — boils down to the tension between freedom and order.

(2006, 46). In Chapter 5, with Ricœur, we'll get a relevant personalist answer to this question. For the time being, we can summarize this with Marja Brouwers' afterword to the translation of More's *Utopia* (2014, 170), as a stepping-stone to the substance of Rousseau's third way: "In earthly policy (*polis*), order is maintained by fear of chaos. Sooner or later, the tensions between freedom and the law will break that order again. Wherever the love of God and neighborly love reign, earthly polis becomes the city of God. There, order is a natural result of freedom, rather than something that is imposed through physical or logical coercion."

The Third Way

The core of Rousseau's third way consists of no longer convulsively avoiding the logic of mimetic desire, as was the case with the former two ways: isolating oneself from others, or blindly and obsequiously obeying the authority that dominates all possible others. With Achterhuis, we recognize in Rousseau's third way the alternative solution of external mediation that René Girard described. It comes down to an impossible choice: "Choose to imitate external examples that we *cannot* compete with, and that *cannot* form an obstacle to desire" (1988, 153). The great world religions already give substance to the third way. In Chapter 5, we'll explore the way non-theistic world views give substance to the third way.

Let us first take a moment to look at Christians, specifically their model, Jesus of Nazareth, whom they aspire to imitate. You cannot compete with Jesus (any more). You cannot view him as an obstacle to the realization of your commitment to others.[70] In describing the third way, I refer to the Christian tradition for a reason. As was demonstrated, this tradition developed in such a way that people realized that they themselves had to take up responsibility in dealing with extreme effects that, as a result of mimetic desire, were translated socially and economically. For this third way, however, we might just as well refer to the Buddhist *Mahayana* tradition (also called "The Great

70 This imitation of Jesus is intensively explored in *The Imitation of Christ* (c. 1418–27) by the mystic Thomas à Kempis, who lived in the transition period from the fourteenth to the fifteenth century.

Vehicle"), in which, in the imitation of Buddha, one does not assert one's happiness individually, as in the *Hinayana* tradition ("The Small Vehicle"), as with the first way of Rousseau, but explicitly creates an opening towards social happiness. Maybe, in a somewhat black-and-white way, we're reminded here of the two paths of jihad. The inner jihad, in imitation of Mohammed, indeed aims at the struggle for the happiness of individuals and society against (mimetic) desires, based upon fasting and prayer. The external jihad, by contrast, surrenders to the collective, just like the second way of Rousseau. The latter is an unimaginable struggle with deep and complex roots against everyone who is against (Islam).

Just as, for a Christian, Jesus is the external model who calls for compassion, and for a Muslim this is Mohammed, for a Buddhist the Buddha is the external model. Jesus, the Buddha and Mohammed all appeal to humans to take up their responsibility.[71]

In Chapter 5, I will elaborate on Rousseau's third way of experiencing freedom, which is described here only briefly, by dealing explicitly with responsibility. I consider the question of freedom and responsibility from both theistic and non-theistic perspectives. So far, from what we have explored above, we can indeed see explicit responsibility imposing itself, a responsibility towards the various victims of an economy that leads to dystopia.

---

[71] See also Jaspers (1962) and Lenoir (2009).

5. From Philosophers of Contract to Philosophers of Responsibility

Agnostic and Atheistic Philosophers of Responsibility

From justice to responsibility[72]

In the search for answers to the questions raised by a society that is seriously plagued by an economy with dystopian features, I shall first focus on the way agnostic and atheist philosophers develop Rousseau's third way, one that leads to responsibility – but without a God as external model. I'm talking about the philosophers who explicitly indicate that one can neither intellectually prove nor disprove the existence of a God, but who emphasize the importance of justice and responsibility with equal passion. Think of agnostic philosophers such as Hume and Kant, but also of atheist philosophers such as Ludwig Feuerbach, Arthur Schopenhauer and Jean-Paul Sartre. All of them arrive at a radical emphasis on the need for man to pursue justice: justice, however, as Feuerbach, Schopenhauer and Sartre all explicitly stated, that is based this time not on a contract that grants full power to the state, but through assuming responsibility. Let us start by describing how agnostic philosophers such as Hume and Kant demonstrated why, in pure philosophical terms, people cannot escape taking each other into account and achieving justice.

For Hume, there are four reasons to emphasize the need for justice. First, man, in order to satisfy his basic needs, relies on collaboration with others. You can't survive as an isolated individual. Furthermore, man only disposes of a relatively limited amount of altruism, as a result of which he'll be quick to accumulate as much as he can, without taking other people into account. Moreover, the supply of goods we need happens to be scarce. This calls for a fair demarcation between

---

72 See also Abicht and Opdebeeck (2016).

that which belongs to one person and that which belongs to another. Finally, human beings have approximately the same basic needs, and consequently, they must ensure an adequately equal satisfaction of these basic needs.

Kant hit explicitly upon the need to legitimize justice when, in his *Critique of Pure Reason*, he declared that we can no longer point to a God to tell us how justice should be shaped by humans. Kant demonstrated that not a single great truth of the philosophy that preceded him could any longer be proven. Not only the existence of God, but also, for example, that of free will. The reason for this was that none of these truths could indeed be perceived empirically. According to Kant, if we hope to arrive at truthful statements about God and more, this empirical perception is necessary to connect to the structure of our intelligence. It is, however, remarkable how Kant brings up the question of God again. It is as if, out of the need for ethics – and more explicitly, for justice – he had to invent God once again.[73] For the fact that Kant demonstrated, from his *Critique of Pure Reason*, that you can prove neither God nor immortality led to sorrow and suicidal thoughts during German Romanticism. Hence a kind of suffering that led back to God.

So Kant reintroduced God – not in the *theological* way that was used by Thomas Aquinas and was, in fact, adopted by Descartes, but from the compelling concept of *justice*. Kant says that justice, which is indispensable for man and society, can, in the last instance, only be guaranteed by a God. For as human beings, we can only experience justice in a limited way during our brief stay on earth. Thus, Kant posits the existence of God neither rationally (along the lines of his epistemology) nor theologically, but *ethically*. And when man desires to be just, that desire consequently demonstrates the necessity of free will.

The atheist Feuerbach, who was born in 1804, the year of Kant's death, comes to the conclusion that man is confronted everywhere with injustice. Man projects the desire for justice on to a non-existing God

---

[73] In broad terms, this is reminiscent of Buddhism, which in principle is not a religion, let alone one that would acknowledge a God. But when it comes to finding a fundamental answer to suffering, a large number of Buddhist interpretations invite you to imagine a warm light during meditation. A light that might heal this suffering and sorrow. See Geurtz (2016).

instead of investigating the structural causes of injustice. Feuerbach's materialist humanism, by contrast, posits the heart of man as the potential source of responsibility. According to Feuerbach, only by devoting our energy to human beings (instead of God) can we help to establish justice.

For Schopenhauer (1788–1860) as well, injustice is intrinsically linked to our world. To him, that world is a blind force. Man's will to live leads him towards self-annihilation, just as, in the movie *La Vita è Bella* ("*Life Is Beautiful*"), Roberto Benigni eagerly barrels down a Tuscan hill in a car without brakes. Therefore, Schopenhauer advocates a philosophical attitude that teaches us to expect less of life, in order to be less disappointed. To achieve this, he, too, ends up relying on the importance of justice, whereby empathy and compassion present themselves.

When we summarize the preceding perspectives, we observe, in the first place, that Hume's philosophical path to articulate justice in principle once again connects with the idea of justice as a virtue. Plato and Aristotle elaborated on the importance of virtues, which was taken over by medieval philosophy before the philosophy of contract emerged. The Reformation, however, abandoned the idea of justice in favour of giving to others what was due to them, within an ethical system of virtues. One moved on to the discourse of an ethics of obligations, starting from what is prescribed in the Bible. In a similar way, Kant worked out the secular version of the ethics of obligations, based upon reason. Later on, as developed in the philosophies of thinkers such as Feuerbach and Schopenhauer, the renewed emphasis on man – as the agent who takes responsibility in order to establish justice – led to the universal declaration of the rights of man in the twentieth century. Which, of course, can only be realized when responsibility is ensured.[74] Let us now take a deeper look at the visions of Marx and Sartre to give shape to the concept of "responsibility".

---

74 For good reason, there also has been a call to approve universal professions of responsibility such as the *Universal Declaration of Human Duties and Responsibilities*, the *Charter of Universal Responsibilities* (http://www.response.org.nz/wp-content/uploads/2012/01/Rio+20-NZ-Rationale-Responsibility-4Jan12.pdf) and the *Charter for Human Responsibilities* (http://www.alliance-respons.net/bdf_fiche-document-178_es.html). See also Opdebeeck (2012).

From communality to responsibility

Marx is the most explicit atheist philosopher of responsibility. His famous remark, that "philosophers have only interpreted the world, in various ways; the point, however, is to change it", is the best expression of this embrace of responsibility. Certainly – in light of the fact that we still associate the ideas of Marx with communism (Rousseau's second way, in the extreme), which reduced everything to common property – his nuanced vision on communality is important. By what he calls "communality", Marx refers to traditional communal rights. A communal right is a right to a community, based on the Latin word *communis*, which we can also recognize in the English word *commons*. The commons in England were initially the land where everyone had the right to cut peat, gather wood, or graze their sheep and goats. Today, one might think of the Tiny Housing movement: people who try to settle down with small, portable, complete but affordable houses (more than a trailer or camper), on grounds that are neither privately owned nor government land, such as a section of forest, or a meadow. Communality means that people may use or enjoy something collectively, without competition tending towards exclusive property (which generates scarcity). We're talking about the enjoyment of equal opportunities with others, instead of a jealousy that is sparked by differences with others.

Achterhuis describes how in Flanders, when the price of the wool rose (around 1500), the communal grounds, or *commons*, were used to graze the sheep, while in England they were turned into private property by enclosures. As a result, the poor there were abandoned to their fate. Marx recalled Thomas More's warning in *Utopia* of how (see Chapter 1) sheep are now so greedy and wild that they devour men. By no longer preserving communality as the context in which to embrace responsibility for the prospects of all, poverty – a scarcity of income – was created.

For Marx, as for Aristotle, man is a communal being. In this, relationships come first. For Marx, communality doesn't just describe common property, but also man as a communal being with responsible relationships – relationships with other people, as well as relationships between people and things, and between people and nature. This is Marx's attempt to avoid reducing either man or nature to victimhood.

Marx concludes that man is engaged in a twofold struggle: one with fellow humans, over scarce commodities, and another with nature, over scarce resources.

Today, Marx's original insight on communality invites us to view communality as an opportunity to shape responsibility within our capitalist system. For example, authors like Michel Bauwens (2013) advocate a form of post-capitalism in which a sharing economy is established.[75] In current terms, this is also called a collaborative economy, or a peer-to-peer economy. Koen Frenken (2016, 4) defines a sharing economy as "the phenomenon that consumers allow one another to make use of their unused goods, potentially for a fee". This happens through internet platform enterprises that can generate the necessary trust between people. At first sight, the sharing economy looks like a new form of the communality following on from Thomas More's "common meadows". Think of the free software Linux, or *Wikipedia*, which everybody can take advantage of, and is entitled to. Yochai Benkler (2004), one of the first advocates of *open source* software such as Linux, uses the term "*sharable goods*", sort of the beginning of what we today call the sharing economy, one which everybody can benefit *from*, but also *to which* everybody can contribute and *for which* everybody can take responsibility. New approaches, like *repair cafés*, where everybody can go to repair their stuff, present an alternative to our throwaway culture that is so damaging to man and the environment. *Co-working spaces* offer new ways to do your office work while sharing the logistics. In each case, we can identify a version of people taking responsibility communally and directly, from peer to peer.

We can find an earlier concrete example of what we today call a sharing economy in the co-operative movements of the late eighteenth century. Through co-operation, consumers as well as producers realized their common goals. Dirk Barrez (2014) is right in his description of the compelling relevance of co-operatives today. The recapturing of the economy Barrez is talking about refers, indeed, to what has always been everybody's property. Co-operation, or collaboration, comes first here, literally and figuratively. This goes all the way to the hard profit sector. Barrez points at Switzerland, where about 70 per

[75] See also Botsman (2010), Mason (2016) and Thackara (2015).

cent of the distribution is in the hands of two co-operative enterprises (*COOP* and *Migros*). Furthermore, he astutely reminds us that, during the 2008–13 economic crisis in Spain, the co-operative enterprise Mondragon not only managed to survive easily, but also raised profits and recruited new personnel. In 2005, Luc Bouckaert, the personalist economist and philosopher, argued already that the rediscovery of the core of the co-operative movement offers a crucial key to the necessary transition of our economy.

Even a brief comparison with the co-operative movements in history teaches us that only when it is built on effective solidarity does today's *Sharing Economy* become the extension of their ideas of communality and responsibility. It is not coincidental that co-operatives are components of what we call a *Social Economy*, which is situated between the private and the public sector, just like communality. And it is no accident that the sharing economy emerged as a social (ecological) sharing economy (today's *repair cafés*, for example). That is why it is important to check how different types of sharing economy might: contain the risk of increasing inequality (for example, wealthy people can increase their income through Airbnb, while such options aren't normally available in social housing); generate a greater burden on the environment (such as when cheaper lodging stimulates more frequent air travel); be disadvantageous to the poor (rents that increase as a result of Airbnb); and encourage discrimination (when people with immigrant backgrounds are not welcome in your Airbnb house). Susie Cagle (2014) even argues that the sharing economy does not restore trust, but that it instead "replicates old patterns of privileged access for some, and denial for others".

Frenken (2016) summarizes the impact of the sharing economy as follows. The economic effects are very positive, but unevenly distributed. The effects on the environment are positive, although less than expected. And the social effects are in fact very complex and potentially negative. Then, as Thomas More put it, the sheep will once again devour people. It's for a good reason that Giana M. Eckhardt and Fleura Bardhi wrote an article in the *Harvard Business Review* (2015) titled "The Sharing Economy Isn't About Sharing at All", in which they argue that when "sharing" is market-mediated – when a company is an intermediary between consumers who don't know each other – it is no longer sharing at all.

Should the present sharing economy boil down to a new recipe for overcoming the most recent crisis of capitalism, we'd still be far from the realization of that which a philosophy of responsibility, or ethical expansion of the economy, aspires to. Some of this reminds us of what we called "instrumental rationality" in Chapter 3: ethical categories, such as the value of sharing among people who have been instrumentalized by the economic system. Roose (2014) states that lots of people are trying to fill holes in their income by monetizing their stuff and their labour in creative ways.[76]

From fear to responsibility

In *L'être et le néant*, Sartre's point of departure, much like a Buddhist's, is the fact that we as human beings are confronted with suffering – one way or another. The fear of this, whether it is fear of suffering a financial bankruptcy or the loss of a loved one, let alone the fear of your own death, brings Sartre to what he calls *une mauvaise foi*, or bad faith. That is, the dismissal of the responsibility that you must assume in your life. Or how, just as at the origins of economy, letting fear dominate risks wiping responsibility off the table.

Actually, in his extension of Rousseau, Sartre also sets out from our fundamental passion for freedom. According to Sartre, however, man risks being of bad faith. Call it a lack of fidelity to his or her yearning for freedom. Rather than formulate answers from a point of freedom to the challenges we encounter on our journey (as we found in Tillich's description of responsibility), we deny this freedom and responsibility out of fear.

However, Sartre refuses to address this fear by means of a religious system (one expression of Rousseau's *third way*), or via an absolute system (Rousseau's *second way*). These denigrate our freedom. That is why Sartre puts freedom first, just like Rousseau. According to Sartre, by setting aside God based upon freedom we acquire our rightful place as responsible human beings. As we saw, Girard actually did something similar. He did this by rejecting the idea of a God who tells us we can slough off our responsibility by offering sacrifices.

---

76 See also Hill (2015).

Theistic Philosophers of Responsibility

Religious existentialism

Exploring Sartre's atheistic existentialism, we can better understand an interesting dichotomy. On the one hand, without an existentialist correction such as Sartre's, Marxism can lead to dogmatism. For Sartre's existentialism holds man – and thus *not* God or the state or a dogma – concretely responsible. On the other hand, when we disconnect Sartre's atheistic existentialism from Marxism, this can generate deeply pessimistic visions, such as those of Heidegger and Jaspers. These philosophers were once again compelled to question the potential for the development of human freedom. It is no surprise, then, that a *religious* existentialism emerged as a reaction to this, from Søren Kierkegaard, among others.

In line with Schopenhauer, however, Kierkegaard at first comes to the conclusion that the world is pointless and suffers from the omnipresence of injustice, in addition to disease, misery and disappointment. Thus, fear also pushes its way to the front with Kierkegaard. However, this fear cannot be abolished simply by according ethics a central position. Clearly, on the basis of the philosophers of contract, the economic path we sketched does not liberate man from his fundamental fear. Therefore, according to Kierkegaard, the surrender to God is important. After the *ethical postulate* of God by an agnostic philosopher such as Kant, here, we are presented with what we might call an *existential postulate*. The existential experience of fear brings us to a leap towards God. Trust in God leads us to the taking up of responsibility. In making this case, Kierkegaard does not lean on theology or the authority of the Church. In Kierkegaard's wake, religious existentialism usually kept its distance from religious institutions such as the Church, for the Church distrusted an individual who assumes responsibility based upon his existential experience.

Mystical responsibility

As with Girard, a Christian interpretation of existentialism emphasizes responsibility based on an imitation of Jesus. As in Rousseau's third way, it concerns the imitation of a role model (Jesus of Nazareth) who calls upon man to efface himself out of compassion for the other.

According to Louis Dupré, this is connected with the distinction already made by Friedrich von Hügel in his work *The Mystical Element of Religion* (1923). The religious hermeneutical experience, including the one upon which a religious philosopher bases himself, can contain three aspects: a rational, an institutional and a mystical one. From a rational point of view, a religious philosopher (just like agnostic philosophers) may emphasize that one can indeed neither prove nor disprove the existence of God. From experience with the institution (the Church), a religious philosopher (such as Girard) may understand that God does not demand sacrifices from man but instead that he assume his responsibility. From mystical experiences, he feels that the urge to take responsibility is most sustainable when you are driven to this by a mystical union with, or trust in, a personal God each time.

Dupré correctly writes that if, in modern times, after all the criticism of the institutional and rational aspects of Christianity there still remain people who are and become Christians, we have to attribute this to the attractive force of the mystical. This keeps fascinating us. With the mystical, von Hügel does not mean the ecstatic, something only a few people experience, nor the magic that an unevolved person all too often confuses with the religious. No, this is about that strange invitation to a new way of being. The religious person does not always want to judge for himself, but to listen to the voice that speaks to him from within (2015, 1,002). The answer he offers articulates an idea very similar to that of responsibility that we explored from a Buddhist perspective earlier.

That is why a Christian existentialist such as Gabriel Marcel (1889–1973) thought that man can proceed further in his thinking than a rational analysis of the problems. He can open himself up to the mystery, because he comes to understand that being is a mystery. Of course, mystique as a foundation is not found only in Christianity (such as with Eckhart), but also in the Kabbalah of Judaism and the Sufism of Islam. In addition to Gabriel Marcel, Augustine in the Middle Ages, Blaise Pascal at the time of the rationalism of Descartes and Søren Kierkegaard are examples of Christian philosophers who arrive at responsibility in this way. Martin Buber and Emmanuel

Levinas are examples of Jewish philosophers who did this from a Jewish point of view.

The Face of the other

In his 1922 book *Ich und Du* (*I and Thou*), the Jewish philosopher Martin Buber (1878–1965) argues that we can only develop our urge for freedom by actualizing our concrete responsibility with regard to a "you". According to Buber, we can only arrive at an authentic dialogue with God when we have engaged, in real life, in a dialogue with the other person. With Buber – in the line of Plato, Thomas More and, as we shall see shortly, Ernst Bloch – we arrive at a plea for the articulation of utopia. Buber isn't dreaming here of a society that cannot be realized (the Greek stem *ou* in "utopia"), but about working towards a good or happy society that has not yet been realized (the other possible Greek stem in "utopia", *eu*, that stands for "good" or "happy").

According to another Jewish philosopher, Emmanuel Levinas (1905–95), lack of responsibility in the economy and society is a consequence of a Western philosophy that started to *grab* reality (in the economy: the employee, nature …) rather than to *grasp* its core. The core of reality is the experience of the other. To take responsibility means to be open to (and respond to) reality instead of grabbing it. Levinas describes our societal situation in a highly current way. The house (*oikos*, or the "eco" in "economy" and "ecology") could be the metaphor for our society here: "I possessed and enjoyed my world as my house. Full of joy for the good of the earth, unaware of the fact that I, though my appropriation of all the good, rendered others poor, deprived them of their rights or even put them to death" (Abicht and Opdebeeck, 2015, 97). Instead of being open to the intrinsic logic of our house (eco-logy), we impose norms upon our house (eco-nomy) that lead to dystopia. Levinas, however, continues: "But someone else rises up in front of me. That is a decisive happening, for something totally new reveals itself …The other presents himself" (Abicht and Opdebeeck, 2015, 97). According to Levinas, we are summoned to responsibility first and foremost by the other. Ethics or responsibility become "la mise en question de ma spontanéité par la présence d'Autrui" ("*the questioning of my spontaneity by the presence of the other*"). Our spontaneous freedom, which is so dear to us, is questioned, perforce demanded by the fact that the other is also there. By extension, we might also include in this other all living beings and nature. When, with Levinas, we do not come close enough to nature, it is fascinating to look to the twentieth-century philosopher Albert Schweitzer (Sartre's cousin). In his ethics of respect for all living beings, he elaborates in a very consistent manner on this notion of expanding the concept of "the other" all the way, to include nature (Van Oyen, 2008).

A Bridge Between Atheistic and Theistic Responsibility

The beginning of this century was marked by religious terrorism all over the world. This forces us constantly to explore the outline of an unavoidable philosophical responsibility, independent of an atheistic or theistic point of view. Ernst Bloch (1884–1977) constructs an interesting bridge between the atheistic and theistic, particularly Christian, philosophers of responsibility. He develops the importance of that which we have already called "concrete utopia". No abstract utopias that make us flee from a harsh and frightening reality, but concrete societal ideas that can be achieved effectively today from an intelligent hope for true freedom. Both atheists and Christians have their responsibility here, Bloch contends in this statement directed at both: "Only an atheist can be a good Christian; only a Christian can be a good atheist."[77] Like Girard, Bloch sheds a traditional religion that stresses the importance of offering sacrifices to God instead of emphasizing the necessity for people to take responsibility. One could, according to Bloch, label a real atheist as a true Christian because he, like Jesus, focuses our attention on man instead of on sacrifices to a God. Moreover, for a true Christian there exists only one authentic God, whereby he, like a true atheist, can renounce everything that is idolatry. Think of the exaltation of gods such as money, technology and economy. Thus, for Bloch, it is clear that both the atheist and the Christian have their individual and societal responsibility (Abicht and Opdebeeck, 2015, 99).

---

[77] A point that is further illustrated in the Afterword to this book.

Paul Ricœur as a Philosopher of Bridges

Paul Ricœur (1913–2005), whom we have already mentioned a few times, is a philosopher of responsibility who arrives at the primacy of responsibility in a rational, philosophical way. Only at the very end of his own philosophical discourse did he refer to Christian discourse as an articulation of responsibility. Ricœur derives responsibility from his thorough study of ethics. Here, we focus on the way in which Ricœur extends his vision of the problem of the fundamentals of ethics[78] to the economy. In what ways can we speak of an institutional translation of responsibility in economic practice?

The desire for happiness more original than suffering

Ricœur starts from the position that man is constituted by an "original affirmation of being", which manifests itself in an attempt and a desire to realize one's happiness. By "original affirmation of being", Ricœur understands the desire for happiness (the act that constitutes our existence) – which precedes our thinking, acting and feeling – as our foundation and guidance. We can view this original affirmation of being as an act of freedom. In fact, it concerns what we are and what we should be. Only in this way is a more authentic life (and a more bona fide life together) beyond alienation possible. Thus, the freedom that Rousseau spoke of is foremost for Ricœur as well.

Ricœur strongly emphasizes the fact that evil, as manifested in suffering and death, is not as original as the act of freedom. According to the author, it is true, though, that evil and freedom clarify one another, and that evil, as in suffering and death, is not only situated at the individual level, but also in the structures within which we operate. Ricœur states this very clearly where he contends that there exists a specific evil in institutions. It concerns the evil of "objectification", as we see it at work in economic dystopia (1968, 27): "One encounters it in all forms of organization. In the division of labor, it takes on the subtle form of a gray and mind-numbing boredom, which gradually consumes the hyper-specialized and monotonous labor." This evil is

---

78 Ricœur (1975) wrote an important contribution to the problem of the foundations of ethics: *Le problème du fondement de la morale.*

often an unfathomable yet unacceptable manifestation of the freedom that makes freedom unattainable for itself.

The invitation to responsibility

When Ricœur posits that his point of departure is the free human being with his desire for and attempt at being happy, according to him, this can only succeed through the encounter with the other. With this acknowledgement of the other as a person, responsibility emerges. We feel called upon or ethically obliged to give and answer to the invitation or challenge by the other. The freedom which started everything, and which we have constantly referred to from Rousseau to Sartre and beyond, is also acknowledged for the other person at hand. So it comes down to letting freedom take shape in inter-subjectivity. As Ricœur sees it, ethical existence as responsibility should be clearly understood as an "option" in which you do (or don't) have respect for the other, as well as for yourself, as a person. You *know* that you only live a dignified life when you promote the person in yourself and in the Other. This option, however, entails that I choose to limit myself, in the sense that I curtail my natural inclination to view everything as the object of my aspirations. It concerns an approach that is usually at odds with the economic one. It is fundamentally important to note here that Ricœur firmly expands this inter-subjective responsibility to the entire world. He reacts against an individualistic ethics, because man is not only an individual but, on the contrary, is constituted within the diverse layers of the "we", rooted in the totality of (economic) structures and institutions.

Responsibility via an institution such as the economy

Should the free human being desire to become fully happy through the responsible encounter with the Other, this is only possible on the basis of responsible institutions. A third moment is necessary, to wit a neutral term, an institution. In principle, an institution ensures that everyone's freedom can be realized without harming the freedom of the Other. Man acts within already existing institutions.

It is, however, remarkable that the tension between freedom and institution can form the basis of a serious contradiction between, on the one hand, the temptation to see freedom as separate from the institution and, on the other, the reality of a bureaucratic institution. With Rousseau, we were pointed here, to the first path (of isolated freedom) and to the second path (of a freedom that has been swallowed by the state). Ricœur argues that humankind threatens to break in two as never before, between, on the one hand, the brief relationships in our friendships, coupledom and private lives, and on the other, the long relationships of social, political and economic life. This central conflict can only be experienced in a sensible way if, deep in your heart, you're strongly convinced of the demand for a synthesis between freedom and the institution. For a freedom that is not institutionalized remains potentially terrorist, and in each institution one has to ask whether it serves the realization and the blossoming of freedom. This is the core question Rousseau posed with his third way: what is a sensible freedom? Ricœur refers to Hegel, who stated that freedoms need to be mediated by familial, legal, economic, social and political institutions.

The question that imposes itself, then, is how ethical rules can be established at the level of institutions. This is because that which comes from the interpersonal realm is so difficult to extend to the institutional level. Ricoeur (1968, 182) states that the social has the tendency to block access to the personal and to *hide* the mystery of interpersonal relationships. The measure for human relations seems to be: "Have we reached individual people?" But we have neither the right nor the power to use this measure. We specifically don't have the right to use this eschatological criterion as a process for preferring "short" relationships at the expense of "long" ones, for in reality, in the latter we practise a love that concerns individual people, even though we are often unaware of this. Ricœur is concerned with the "short" relationships among individuals and the "long" relationships that run through the institutions. He points to the profound and hidden unity of all these relationships. Hence the great importance that he attaches to justice. Ricoeur sees justice as the institutional instrument that enables different freedoms to coexist. In his 1990 book *Soi-même comme un autre*, Ricœur elaborates on this thesis in line with Aristotle, by emphasizing the link between justice and equality, which we will explore more deeply in Chapter 6.

A Buddhist Philosophy of Responsibility

Responsibility in Buddhist terms

Let us now consider how responsibility looks from a Buddhist perspective. Ricœur's transition from the individual to the institutional reminds us at first sight of the relationship between the Small and the Great Vehicle, to which we'll return next. Buddhism as a source for the articulation of responsibility has the advantage that, whether you view Buddhism as a religion or not, it is just as much also a philosophy. It's really about a philosophy that has developed into a religion. Think of the statues of Buddha that are displayed for adoration. However, Buddhism as a religion is only rarely associated with terrorism or violence. An important advantage of the Buddhist philosophy of responsibility is the fact that its way of dealing with suffering or dystopia is strongly comparable with atheistic as well as theistic philosophies of responsibility (see also the end of Chapter 3). The essence that this comes down to is always taking responsibility through compassion.

Just as has gradually happened with us in the West since Modernity, in Buddhism man, instead of a God, was made responsible for avoiding the various dystopian effects that we suffer from. Buddhism – as the foundation of Bhutanese or Japanese society, for example – is pre-eminently a philosophy that denounces the offering of sacrifices to the gods (as in Hinduism), just as Girard questioned the offering of sacrifices in Christianity. The human Buddha realized that he himself was responsible for facing his fears and the suffering and unrest these entailed. In his second law of nature, Hobbes advanced the golden rule. This comes down to treating others in the way you want to be treated. The Buddha develops this law of nature into a plea for compassion.

Guanyin, or Buddhist compassion, in the economy[79]

Let us take a brief look at the literal application of compassion as the basis of economic management in Japan. Japan is a country that in the last decades has eminently suffered from a number of negative economic effects: from burnouts and suicides in the business world to extreme effects on nature, such as in Fukushima.

---

[79] See also Opdebeeck and Habisch (2011a).

The renowned Japanese camera company Canon got its name from the Buddhist bodhisattva *Guanyin* ("Kannon", in Japanese, previously transliterated in English as "Kuanyin", "Kwannon" or "Kwanon"). The term *Canon* sounded more familiar in English, and was adopted in 1935. *Guanyin* is the name of the Buddhist goddess of compassion. The name was chosen as an expression of the company's mission to produce cameras as a concrete gesture of compassion towards the world. To let as many people as possible enjoy the fact that they could record important events on film. The original *Guanyin* logo even contained a picture of the goddess of compassion. You see her with countless arms and hands, as a metaphor of an extreme compassion for people. The compassion that the Japanese company aspired to, from its mission towards society, is a concrete example of what we have already described as the Great Vehicle, the Mahayana, in Buddhism. In fact, the Mahayana does not focus on personal enlightenment as a goal in itself, as in the Hinayana (the Small Vehicle) tradition. In the Mahayana, it is essential that every living being can eventually attain enlightenment.

When someone lives his life according to this ideal, then in Buddhist terms he or she is a *bodhisattva*. Hence, a responsible company manager in Japan, Bhutan or elsewhere is a bodhisattva. In the West, we might call such a responsible manager spiritually inspired. Compare this with the mission statement of the sporting goods company Decathlon as it appears on its website. Using almost the same terminology as Canon, Decathlon declares that it "wants to make sports accessible to everyone". In formulating its values, responsibility (or what it calls "generosity" and "compassion") is central. It is no surprise that the founder of Decathlon, Michel Leclercq, was strongly influenced by the twentieth-century personalist philosopher André Rochais, who was closely connected with Paul Ricœur's philosophy of responsibility.

Beyond sustainability

It is interesting to note that the Buddhist discussion of responsibility as compassion goes beyond the concept of sustainability that has become mainstream in the meantime. When you extend sustainability to include compassion, you transcend the view of sustainability that dictates that, as an entrepreneur, you only take employees, the developing world or the environment into account to the degree that your personal advantage, such as company profits, is not fundamentally endangered. Or to put it more concretely, sustainability in the business world is often nothing more than window dressing, according to which you only do something out of "ethical" considerations for employees, the developing world or the environment if it eventually generates benefits for you. In the showcase or on your website (the window), some things are presented more attractively than they actually are in reality. We can understand this even better by again involving the difference between the Mahayana (the Great Vehicle) and the Hinayana (the Small Vehicle) traditions in Buddhism. Starting from the Hinayana, you are above all focused on your own interests. The Mahayana clearly looks beyond that. Crucial historical events or evolutions such as Fukushima or the climate crisis can provide an incentive to rediscover the tradition of the Great Vehicle. Or they can, in general, provide an incentive for expanding our concept of sustainability as compassion. In English, one might try out the neologism "mercy-ability" instead of sustainability. Then we would stop thinking of the burnt-out employee, the poor in the South and the environment as victims of the economic system only when this suits us as window dressing. Only when we stop doing this can we rediscover economy as a source of compassion, blessings, gifts, let's say happiness. It is important to realize how, starting from Mahayana Buddhism, this compassion from an employer is concretely developed through "*paramitas*": virtues such as insight, patience, caring, generosity and, not least, justice. Each of these is an essential key for the development of an economy of happiness, expressed as Gross National Happiness.

Gross National Happiness

Beyond the Gross National Product

Let us now take a more detailed look at the Gross National Happiness that originated in Bhutan and which we have been referring to since the Introduction to this book.[80]

---

80 For a detailed overview, see *Provisional Findings of 2015 Gross National Happiness Survey*, Centre for Bhutan Studies & GNH Research, Timphu, 2015. See also the Centre's website: http://www.bhutanstudies.org.bt/

As we discussed, it was Singye Wangchuck, the father of the current king of Bhutan, who brought happiness in his country to the forefront in 1972. He refused to tie the policies of his Himalayan kingdom to the quest for ever more economic growth. As of 9 September 1979, this was translated into the concept of Gross National Happiness, when he told journalists in Bombay that "Gross National Happiness is more important than Gross Domestic Product" (Provisional Findings, 2015, 1). Since then, GNP (Gross National Product) as a measure of governance was replaced by GNH (Gross National Happiness). The Centre for Bhutan Studies is responsible for this, and back in 2004 it organized the first international conference on GNH. In 2010, they began measuring GNH every five years. In fact, the former king of Bhutan (and now his son, Jigme Khesar Namgyel Wangchuck, the present king) aligned himself with the book of law that was created when the unification of Bhutan took place, at the beginning of the eighteenth century. In that book, we read that, if the government cannot guarantee the happiness of the people, it has forfeited its right to exist: "If the government cannot create happiness for its people, then there is no purpose for government to exist" (2015, 1). In this sense, it is not surprising that, in order to guarantee that happiness, the king decided in 2006 to further relinquish his power by fully establishing democracy. This led to the first elections in 2008. Article 9 of Bhutan's first constitution after these elections states that the government must work on this national happiness in several diverse fields: "The Government shall … provide good governance, and ensure peace, security, well-being and happiness of the people" (2015, 1). The themes of the first international conference on GNH in 2004 and the most recent conference of 2015 emphasized the importance of converting the idea of GNH into practice: "Operationalizing Gross National Happiness" and "From GNH to Praxis and Policy". The latest democratic elections in Bhutan took place in July 2013. For the first time, the People's Democratic Party gained power. While the new prime minister leaves the task of promoting the GNH idea internationally to the King and the Centre for Bhutan Studies, the elected government also concentrates on strengthening the GNH in Bhutan itself.

A globalized phenomenon

At the international GNH conference, in the fall of 2015, Bhutan ascertained that its idea of a GNH had gone remarkably global. It was no longer just the world that was fascinated by this tiny principality's vision and practice of happiness, but now it was also Bhutan that invited hundreds of people from other parts of the world to learn from diverse, global expertise on societal happiness. At the beginning of this book, we mentioned the *Human Development Index*, developed by Martha Nussbaum and Amartya Sen in the 1990s. This index already paid attention to human development from a broad perspective. However, things accelerated after an appeal from European Commission President José Manuel Barroso at the Beyond GDP conference in 2007 to devise new metrics in addition to Gross National Product. Also important was the 2008 initiative by the French President Nicolas Sarkozy to set up the Commission on the Measurement of Economic Performance and Social Progress, together with authorities such as Joseph Stiglitz and Sen. The result was, among other things, the OECD's *Better Life Index* of 2011 enabling the comparison of international welfare results. Since September 2013, GNH has been listed as a new economic paradigm on the United Nations map. At that time, Bhutan delivered a report entitled *Happiness: Towards a New Development Paradigm* to the UN General Assembly. This was done in line with UN resolution 65/309, which was approved unanimously by the UN in July 2011, under the title *Happiness: Towards a holistic approach to sustainable development*. Another striking expression of the GNH concept was the *World Happiness Report* in 2012, from authors such as Jeffrey Sachs and Richard Layard, already mentioned in the Introduction. In the latest edition of this report, the effects of income and wealth inequality on happiness are also taken into account. During the last ten years, there has been a significant increase in inequality in the world with regard to the experience of happiness. In the introduction to this latest edition, Sachs therefore states avowedly: "This report gives evidence on how to achieve societal well-being. It's not by money alone, but also by fairness, honesty, trust and good health. The evidence here will be useful to all countries as they pursue the new *Sustainable Development Goals*." Sustainable Development Goals

(SDGs), launched in 2015, are the successor to the UN's Millennium Development Goals (MDGs) (from 2000) that had focused primarily on poverty. Within these sustainable development goals, as we saw in Bhutan, other dimensions have seen concrete progress: in health, education, sustainable cities and communities, responsible ecological use, peace and justice, etc. As early as September 2010, Jigme Thinley, then the Prime Minister of Bhutan, had already proposed adding happiness as an additional Millennium Development Goal.

Linking values to responsibility and meaningfulness

In their publications on national happiness, the Belgian writers Maarten Desmet (2013) and Peter[81] Van Rompuy (2016) emphasize that, in Bhutan's concept of GNH, they see the emergence of values that are also deemed important in the West. Van Rompuy summarizes the core of these values under a concept he calls the quality of life in our society. For Desmet, the GNH is a philosophy of development that attempts to take into account values within a society and the way those values contribute to the well-being of that society (51). For him, the most important values in the GNH are holism, collectivity, sustainability and justice (45). The holistic approach demands the mapping of as many as possible of the elements of our complex society that are concerned with happiness and that cannot be reduced to a Gross National Product. The collective is based on the common goal of ensuring that we take each other and the planet into account in a sustainable way. Thus, the collective implies sustainability. It means to act in such a way that you take into account the earth as well as the (future) living beings who live on it. Justice as a value that can shape the GNH comes down to everybody's right to happiness. Access to education and healthcare are expressions of this. Interestingly, in Bhutan, in view of the measuring of the GNH, these values are turned into reality in nine measurable dimensions. These concern health (physical as well as mental), upbringing (the passing down of values, education), culture (participation in and correct mastery of their native language, in addition to the official English), the use of time (the equilibrium between labour and life), good governance (political

[81] Peter Van Rompuy is the son of Herman Van Rompuy who wrote the Foreword to this book.

participation, fundamental rights, a solidly functioning government), communal life (social contacts, family quality, volunteer work, safety, charity), the standard of living (income, wealth, housing), ecological diversity (environmental responsibility, urban versus rural life) and, last but not least, psychological well-being (satisfaction, the experiencing of spirituality).

The question now is how the *quality of life* Van Rompuy talks about, or the *values* that he and Desmet both hold out, have a real chance to be effectively realized in society. Here, taking responsibility (for policymaking) appears to be crucial. Desmet rightly argues that we arrive at the taking up of responsibility: "Whichever path the GNH will go down nationally and internationally, something has been launched – a plea for responsibility" (2013, 84).

Nor should it be taboo to articulate the question of meaningfulness, specifically to shape this responsibility effectively. Hence the more complete definition of the GNH developed by Desmet: "Gross National Happiness measures the quality of a country and posits that when material and spiritual development come together and strengthen each other, positive development takes place" (2013, 51). This definition, in which the importance of spirituality is emphasized, dovetails with the point of view of the present king of Bhutan: "Gross National Happiness measures the quality of a country in a more holistic way and believes that the beneficial development of human society takes place when material and spiritual development occurs side by side to complement and reinforce each other" (Provisional Findings, 2015, 1).

But what does spirituality actually mean in Bhutan? The official documents do not beat around the bush, stating that spirituality boils down to Buddhist compassion: "Spirituality can be defined as compassion" (Provisional Findings, 2015, 3). And: "The indispensable core of spirituality is the cultivation and manifestation of compassion" (2015, 3). In Bhutan, this spirituality goes hand in hand with politics, provided that the government actually embodies this: "A convergence between politics and spirituality cannot be controversial if spirituality is at the heart of governance" (2015, 3). However, these words need to be followed by acts: "Anyone who claims that there is a road to enlightenment without practicing compassion is lying outright" (2015,

3). At the same time, despite its deep Buddhist inspiration, spirituality in Bhutan is developed in an actively pluralistic manner and is not linked exclusively to a single religion: "Spirituality does not necessarily mean following a particular religion or a particular school of religion as a whole. It does not exclude plural identities" (2015, 3).[82]

Measuring Gross National Happiness

What is most striking in the latest GNH metrics in Bhutan, compared to the results of 2010? On the basis of the Alkire Foster (AF) method (a flexible, context-shaped technique for measuring poverty and well-being), around 7,000 respondents (out of a population of about 700,000) were surveyed, using some 150 questions that cover the nine value dimensions mentioned above. Since the survey of 2010, GNH rose almost 2 per cent. It is notable, though, that this rise was mostly determined by factors that normally also influence the rise of Gross National Product, such as an improved standard of life, an increase in services, more housing and healthcare, and an increase in things like the number of tickets to cultural events. As these factors are most prevalent in cities, there is also an increase in the number of city people who are happy and a decrease in the number of happy rural people.

However, what is especially striking in the GNH measurements in Bhutan in 2015 is the fact that psychological well-being dropped significantly, compared with the previous measurement in 2010: "Spirituality significantly decreased" (Provisional Findings, 2015, 65). In the first place, this means that the average Bhutanese experiences himself as less spiritual than in previous times. Asked whether spirituality was of great importance to them personally, 44 per cent of the respondents said yes in 2015, while in 2010 it was more than half. At the same time, we see emotions like fear gaining importance: "Emotions like selfishness, jealousy, anger, fear and worry significantly increased" (2015, 65). These are the very emotions that we discussed at the beginning of this book as being the basis of an economy that risks sliding into dystopia. It is remarkable that this trend is mirrored

[82] For more on the interwoven nature of spirituality and (economic) politics, and the personalist Jacques Maritain's insights on this, see Abicht and Opdebeeck (2015), pp. 85–6.

in other dimensions, such as community life. The degree to which citizens feel involved with the local community decreases from 70 to 64 per cent. And trust in one's neighbours (which, as we've seen, is crucial to establishing meaningfulness) has decreased during the last five years. In 2010, 45 per cent claimed to trust most of their neighbours, but in 2015 this dropped to 25 per cent. The percentage of volunteer work has also dropped, as has the number of charitable donations (not unimportant in Buddhist culture). Attention to the *Driglam Namzha*, Bhutan's official code of etiquette, and to the whole set of norms through which traditions manifest themselves in clothing and architecture, has fallen from 60 to 43 per cent. And sense of responsibility towards the environment dropped by 5 per cent. At the same time, satisfaction with the government has decreased enormously. This may well be linked to the fact that democracy was established in 2008, just before the 2010 survey, and as a result satisfaction with and gratitude towards the government was running high at the time. Now, of course, you can also see the downsides of democracy. On the positive side, gender inequality is decreasing, as more and more women are beginning to consider themselves happy, though the imbalance is still large: 51 per cent of men consider themselves happy, while only 39 per cent of women do (2015, 68).

At the GNH conference in the Fall of 2015, the president of the Centre for Bhutan Studies (CBS) correctly argued that people will have to monitor this development closely and take appropriate measures if they hope to avoid losing the uniqueness of Bhutan, where GNH takes priority over GNP: "The 2015 GNH Index provides a self-portrait of a society in flux, and offers Bhutanese the opportunity to reflect on the direction society is moving, and make wise and determined adjustments." It was no coincidence that an appeal was issued to the numerous young Bhutanese who attended the 2015 GNH conference to keep the utopian character of Bhutan alive: "Bhutan needs your wisdom and your idealism. Even, we need your innocence and ability to dream things that others think are impossible. Please feel invited to our common project of building GNH."

The economy in search of meaningfulness

Peter Van Rompuy (2016) finds it problematic that, although Bhutan has chosen to put human happiness at the centre, it hasn't opted for economic growth in order to guarantee this: "The temptation to apply ourselves only to happiness is great. We can stay perfectly happy without these few little percentages of extra economic growth, right?" (2016, 69). Van Rompuy casts Bhutan in stark contrast to Japan. In Japan, economic growth was allegedly given carte blanche, resulting in neglect for human happiness (depressions, suicides). Apart from the fact that the above-mentioned Japanese *Guanyin* case puts things clearly into perspective, Van Rompuy paints a one-sided picture of Bhutan's GNH project, one of pretty but unrealistic intentions: "The king of Bhutan was a man with noble intentions" (2016, 69). So Van Rompuy interprets the latest elections in 2013 as a reckoning with this so-called option for happiness, given the neglect of economic growth: "The Bhutanese population clearly thought that happiness cannot be separated from prosperity. You cannot build a paradise of happiness in an economic graveyard" (2016, 70). And he even takes it a step further: "Europe must not become an oversized Bhutan" (2016, 70). As a result, all kinds of things that are important to people, like pensions and social security, would come to a halt.

However, on the basis of the figures from the Centre for Bhutan Studies, it is clear that it is incorrect to assert that Gross National Happiness in Bhutan before the newly installed government of 2013 hadn't contributed even a small amount to the Gross National Product. On the contrary: during the period from 2010 to 2015, which was in fact still dominated by the previous government, they achieved economic growth of between 3.6 and 6.8 per cent (without counting the exceptional growth years 2010 and 2011, with growth figures of 9.32 and 10.06 per cent respectively).[83] These are growth figures which Europe (in that period) can only envy. The problem in Bhutan is not failing to grow economically, but rather the fact that the happiness behind the GNH is threatened. The GNH includes

[83] Source: World Bank (https://data.worldbank.org/country/bhutan). Compare this with data from the Asian Development Bank (https://www.adb.org/countries/bhutan/economy).

the most important categories that also increase GNP: investments, production, healthcare, up to and including education and culture. Happiness is not threatened because of declines in specific categories. It is, rather, the opposite, as we indicated. Happiness declined owing to the development of dimensions that are not included in a classical GNP. Think of psychological well-being, including the experience of spirituality and control over emotions such as fear and jealousy. But community life, trust, volunteer work and environmental responsibility also declined. This suggests that when you try to establish a concrete economic utopia in a country like Bhutan, there is a risk that the afore-mentioned classical contradiction between economy and ethics will resurface. The problem is not so much growing the economy itself, but rather combining it with the simultaneous rise of happiness.

Peter Van Rompuy then comes to a conclusion: "The example of Bhutan shows that a policy of happiness is only sustainable when employment and welfare are also created. The example of Japan shows that welfare can only be sustainable when it isn't at the expense of happiness." As if we are currently witnessing the rise of the impossible utopia in Bhutan and of the economic dystopia in Japan. While this might be correct for Japan, the explanation above showed that present-day Bhutan is not an impossible utopia, but a concrete utopia. Day by day, they are trying to continue to build on this concretely by taking hold, each time anew, of that which is crucial to transcend the contradiction between utopia and dystopia (as has transpired from the approach of Bhutanese youth). You can summarize this under psychological well-being in the broad sense, whereby trust prevails over fear and jealousy. This is expressed in the taking of responsibility, in community work, volunteer work and environmental behaviour. Precisely by solidifying this psychological well-being, the Bhutanese prevent "prosperity and happiness from growing too far apart", to use Van Rompuy's words (2016, 76). But for this, we do not have to look for a new equilibrium "somewhere between Bhutan and Japan", as Van Rompuy puts it. It is the equilibrium that was found long ago in Bhutan, one that can inspire the West, with adjustments based on the latest metrics.

According to Van Rompuy, the balance necessary to transcend the utopia of happiness as well as the dystopia of excessive economic growth comes down to what he calls "the quality of life". He is convinced that quality of life can be "an adequate foundation ... to shape an economy on a human scale". We have, however, shown that quality of life is more a result of taking responsibility in the economy than the basis for an economy where people are central. The foundation of this responsibility, and therefore of this quality of life, lies in what we have called "psychological well-being", using Bhutan's language for GNH. In line with the philosophers and practices of responsibility that we explored earlier, taking responsibility effectively is based on trust. Perhaps Van Rompuy has a similar point in mind when, at the end of his book, he develops a separate piece about the necessity of *drive*. He writes: "People only get a 'drive' when they feel that they're part of a project that transcends them" (2016, 119). In this sense, Bhutan is more an example of a successful, concrete utopia than of what Van Rompuy would probably call a failed utopia. The "quality of life" that concerns Van Rompuy is, in fact, a description of what is called Gross National Happiness in Bhutan. In line with the aforementioned Stiglitz commission, Van Rompuy correctly describes this quality of life as "a broader concept than just economic production and a standard of living. It embraces the total spectrum of factors that determine what we consider valuable in our life and is not restricted to the material aspects." This quotation could almost have come straight from the report of GNH metrics in Bhutan in 2015. The eight important dimensions of the intended quality of life that Van Rompuy discusses in his book are variations not only of the Stiglitz report, but also of the dimensions of GNH in Bhutan that we described earlier, with the exception of what we have called "psychological well-being". In fact, Peter Van Rompuy admits this shortcoming in his vision when he compares some of his findings with Eurostat's *Quality of Life* index for Europeans from 2015: "In this context, it makes sense to use the above eight indicators, plus one: satisfaction in life, or happiness" (2016, 81).

6. Economic Responsibility

What is the ultimate meaningfulness behind our tremendous desire for economy? That is the question we asked ourselves at the beginning of this book. Humans will always remain tempted to practise economy, but what is the sense of this when the dystopia of economic doom and gloom prevails over the utopia of milk and honey? In the heart of Chapter 5, where we surveyed the foundations of the economy, it became clear that (created) scarcity determines not just the research parameters of economic science but, simultaneously, also the victims of economic practice. For example, we think of people with burn-out on the shop floor, the poor among us and in the South, and the environment. In fact, in each case, we're actually dealing with a variation of scarcity: a scarcity of job satisfaction, not enough money for the poor in our countries, a lack of means in poor countries, not enough biodiversity in nature, and, last but not least, as we have just established, a dearth of meaningfulness for contemporary man. From its theoretical presuppositions, such as presenting our needs as infinite, in practice the economy itself appears to create victims every time, which expresses itself in one form of scarcity or another.

Thus, we are invited again and again to contemplate the presuppositions, the points of departure, of our economy. Today, it proves to be irresponsible and pointless to just continue developing complex economic models and policy decisions based on these presuppositions. In this chapter, starting from the philosophers and practices of contract and responsibility that we explored earlier, we want to examine how we can see these presuppositions being shifted, inverted with a view to the happiness of man. But first, let us review the crucial points of departure at the core of the present-day economy, which is leading us towards dystopia.

Interim Review: The Core of Today's Economy

The economy as a box of blocks

A first point of departure in the current economy is what you might call a kind of "building bucket" presupposition. A presupposition that seems a little strange at first, but is fundamentally important because of its consequences for the other presuppositions. For in order to construct their theory, economists consider a series of economically important data as given and indisputable. This allows them, as with building blocks, to work out various models and decisions. One such assumed given is that our human needs are infinite. The state of nature is also considered a given in an economic model, just as are, for example, the quality of labour in a particular country, the level of the technology and the amount of capital available. In other words, this concerns the various potential data points, or building blocks, that we must consider in order to shape our economy. From the first class in economics, the young economist will as it were be handed this bucket of building blocks. He is reassured that the ethical side of the question will be dealt with in the ethics course, as we saw at the beginning of this book. These data points, these building blocks, form a circle around the economic events from which the economist may pick elements at will. Thanks to this circle of data, you don't have to take responsibility for important elements like our essential human needs, nature, the quality of labour, technology, or the world of finance. Fortunately, people are gradually starting to realize this. In fact, this connects with the critiques of John Maynard Keynes in his *General Theory* on models that were based on unrealistic presuppositions.

It is noteworthy that the entire social current that is driving transition in the economy was in fact unleashed when people began to question the consequences of this "building-blocks bucket" presupposition, specifically with regard to the "environmental block" in this bucket. What is the sense of an economic science that proclaims our needs to be infinite and promotes exploiting our ecosystem at will? Since the 1970s, the Club of Rome and books like E. F. Schumacher's *Small Is Beautiful* (1973) have warned us of the danger that, by accepting these presuppositions, we risk bartering away the very living environment of the world where we have ended up as human beings – our first world. Immediately we see that, with this first presupposition, we are already creating environmental scarcity. From the beginning of the development of economic activities (explicitly with industrialization), the environment has often been the victim, sacrificed to unilateral economic growth.

The individual first

A second fundamental point of departure in the economy that regularly surfaced in previous chapters states that the individual comes first. For instance, when purchasing something, an individual customer decides whether a part of his or her infinite needs have been met: thus, whether he or she has been ostensibly satisfied. The individual gets carte blanche to compare the usefulness of a commodity or a service with the usefulness of another commodity or service. As such, mimetic desire also plays a role here. Thus, under the influence of this presupposition of individuality, terms such as "economic activity" and "uneconomic activity" were unilaterally subjectively tinted. An action is viewed as uneconomic when it doesn't yield an advantage to those who seek this action. The question of whether or not a particular initiative produces happiness for the entire community is all too quickly neglected.

As a result, today's economy is making us lose more and more of the meaningfulness of being, of working and living together with others. In the context of the competitive struggle on a global scale, solidarity and compassion become a liability and unbearable cost for the enterprise. This contributes to the loss of value of the common interest. Priority is accorded to individual projects (my training), individual survival strategies (my job and income) and individual goods (my house, my car, my newspaper) as the fundamental and irreplaceable expression of freedom. The person is overlooked. The logic of economic competition is elevated as the obligatory logic of society as a whole, which unavoidably leads to a battle of interests between employers and employees, to burn-out and harassment on the job, etc.

After the gap with nature, earth (our first world), we thus collide into the gap with our second world. We're confronted with the world of the Other from the moment we are born on this earth: my mother, my father, my partner and my child, my colleague, client, patient, the poor, the foreigner, the disabled person, etc. By unilaterally putting man as individual on the throne in the economy, we risk neglecting, objectifying and victimizing the person.

Scarcity in itself

The confrontation with scarce resources in the traditional economic sense is the opposite of the (ostensibly infinite) needs of man in the economy. Thus, the economy is delegated the task of investigating that aspect of human behaviour that asserts itself when, while striving to satisfy his infinite needs, man is confronted with scarce means and resources.

The presupposition of infinite human needs is clearly linked to not wanting to acknowledge the meaningful possibility of restraining our needs instead of letting them grow unabated. This is the systematic cultivation of greed and desire that we sketched, as a result of which, among other things, the gap with our Third World is constantly widening. In this sense, the truth of the famous saying by Mahatma Gandhi is self-evident: "The world has enough for everyone's need, but not enough for everyone's greed." This prophetic statement is scientifically proven today: technically, we can solve the problem of hunger across the globe. Only the political-economic choice and the will are lacking. In the economic process, this amplification of needs is of course strongly encouraged by unfettered, non-selective advertising. It is certain that advertising does not stimulate us to restrain our needs. All too often, advertisers abuse their position of enormous power, while they could just as well play the opposite role, discouraging instead of boosting our needs.

Specifically with regard to the poorest countries in the South, it becomes obvious that the creation of artificial scarcity here in the West, in addition to their still-dire scarcity of basic needs (e.g. food and water), is a serious problem. A gap with our Third World is created. The ever-increasing inequality on the global scale makes the South the pre-eminent victim.

The end justifies the means

The next point of departure in our economy is the systematic division of ends and means. With this presupposition, economics often give preference to the means instead of the ends. The result of this is that ethical freedom and the potential of man to choose the goals he ultimately prefers are threatened. Moreover, there is little room for a viewpoint whereby, in pursuit of man's happiness, that which is chosen as a means (labour or machines) in one situation may be chosen *as an end in itself* in another.

Meaningful, qualitatively rich labour could be put forward as an end, an objective, in itself. The economic logic of abolishing as much labour as possible in favour of (cheaper) machines or robots, however, is anchored in the idea that labour is simply labelled under *means of production* and not as a potential *end or goal in itself.* The same is, in fact, true of machines. These too are rarely viewed as an end in themselves, in the sense of us specifically aspiring to machines that are friendly to people and the environment. Just as long as they're as cost-efficient as possible.

Starting from this fourth presupposition, one can, among other things, explain the gap with what we could call a Fourth World in the West. For the replacement of simple labour by advanced technology partly results in ever-larger segments of native and immigrant populations being unemployed. These are the poor among us. Partly because of the constant pressure for cost savings, and because of the recent wave of refugees, this trend is not likely to end on its own.

The centrality of utility

In the economy, one does not bother asking why specific products or services are pursued. The economy doesn't have to pay attention to the qualitative difference between meaningful and meaningless products or services. That is the business of ethics. What is really important is the quantitative effect of the choice. Namely: does or doesn't the merchandizing of this commodity or service lead to usefulness and profit?

A consequence of putting such priority on utility maximization is that, in the economy, focus is centred on the short term, not the long term. Keynes put it like this: "In the long run, we're all dead." One has to observe closely and react rapidly. Just think of the facial expressions of stockbrokers who are reacting as quickly as they can to changing stock prices. This presupposition of usefulness is maybe most pronounced in the financial world, with its constant attempts to turn $1 into $2 as quickly as possible. It is striking to note how much politics here has been displaced by finance. The financial markets were allowed to exert control over money outside of politics. This happened against the background of a permanent and growing divergence between the "financial-economic" and "real-economic" realms. Only a small fraction of current financial transactions is still in the service of the creation of real new wealth. The rest is purely speculative.

This creates the gap between the financial world and the real world, or between the financial economy and the real economy. The victim here is the real world of, for example, people without a job, of insufficient care for people in the margins, and inadequate investments in education, art and culture.

And finally, prices

In the economy we have described, it soon became apparent that there was a need for a system to co-ordinate the respective preferences of people in demand and supply. Those who seek usefulness who rationally use means to reach the stated goals quickly find themselves in need of something like prices. Prices are an expression of the (relative) scarcity (of goods and services). This is how demand and supply effectively become possible in the market.

The economy is thus based on the convergence of market and self-interest. The market mechanisms boil down to the channelling of individualism and irresponsibility into socially accepted structures. A plane ticket from Paris to Venice, for example, that is many times cheaper than the ecologically more justified train ticket (at night) to the same destination.

In general, neither buyer nor seller is responsible for anything except for him- or herself. A rich seller is acting "uneconomically" when he sells at lower prices to financially weaker persons. Only during the romantic Christmas season do we find exceptions to this: (business) people who occasionally make a gesture. A rich buyer will not pay more just because he is dealing with a relatively poor supplier. The exception of people who consciously buy their coffee or bananas in a fairtrade shop confirms the rule here again. Normally speaking, when imported goods are cheaper, a buyer will not choose the more expensive domestic products.

Everything can be expressed in prices and is thus for sale. As a result, people become more and more estranged from those things in life that cannot have a price, if they care to remain authentic. Actually you cannot put a price, for example, on solidarity and compassion with elderly people or the disabled. Or on trust in people, and especially in the transcendent. The fact that trust, compassion and, certainly, transcendence have been relegated in recent years to the realm of taboo creates a chasm in our world of meaningfulness. The spiritual father of the Flemish Green party, Luc Versteylen (1981), once called this "the zero world" (next to the five other worlds mentioned). A so-called *zero* world because our society believes it's OK to dump it. The present-day philosopher Roger Scruton states that the *Lebenswelt* is cleared of all bonds of pious obedience that cannot be replaced by self-created obligations or obligations of free will: "The world is transformed without reference to the transcendental, without the encounter with sacred matters, without the vows of trust" (2016, 37).

Justice and Transcending the Tension between Dystopia and Utopia

The question we have arrived at after the interim review we have just concluded is: to what degree can we still speak of attention to the victims of the economic activity whom we see emerging in our worlds: nature as our first world, concrete people around us in our second world, the poor in our Third World countries (in the South) and in what we called the Fourth World here, our real (fifth) world and, last but not least, meaningfulness, or what we understood by our "zero world"? Or, as the central question in this book is formulated: to what extent can we transcend dystopia?

Among the philosophers of contract, it was *justice* that proved to be the pre-eminent ethical term to keep dystopia away from our economic doings and dealings: "Power and revenue are being centralized into large companies like Apple and Alibaba, but responsibility and risk are being devolved onto us as individuals … There are many important consequences of that polarization, and they reach a very fundamental level of human existence, where we rightly begin to invoke philosophical principles like fairness and justice" (2015, 10). Most of the philosophers of responsibility also relied on justice. That is why we briefly return to this philosophical background. With the philosophers of contract, justice was served by concluding a contract, with a special role for the state. With the philosophers of responsibility, justice was always shaped by responsibility. By grasping an even more precise justice as the common basis to fall back on for both philosophers of contract and of responsibility, we aim to examine how the presuppositions of the economy can now be rephrased with a view to transcending dystopia.

In the previous chapters, it became clear that the social justice we are talking about here is the moral quality that allows citizens or the government to grant to another person, with a kind of self-evidence, that which he is entitled to as a human being, if one aspires to walk righteously through life. Hidden within this "granting or not granting", there is an important cause of the tension between utopia and dystopia. To think that you can really guarantee everyone in this world a subsistence income is a utopia. The opposite of this is a dystopia. You can effectively grant the other that which he is entitled to through a contract or through responsibility. Justice does not only deal with property, commodities and the flow of money, but with all the values that people can realize with and for one another, such as safety, health, freedom and life itself.

Merits versus needs

Two possible points of departure or principles of social justice play an important role in the economy, to wit: "*to each according to his merits*" (a fair day's wage) and "*to each according to his needs*". The first principle can be honoured through a contract. The second one soon becomes an appeal to responsibility. By putting merits first, the aim is to increase economic production by stimulating performance, thus realizing the greatest utility. The concept of merit has various meanings, such as performance, endeavour, and so on. Furthermore, "*to each according to his merits*" always refers to the past. For merit is based on a skill, a degree, knowledge, or productivity acquired (usually unequally) in the past. As a result, this criterion of fairness based on merit tends towards inequality. Just think of the phenomenon of the unequal income distribution. People are born with an unequal distribution regarding intelligence, which in part determines the degrees and income earned. In this sense, the distribution of income is a kind of reflection of the unequal distribution of intelligence and culture.

In the second important principle of justice, "*to each according to his needs*", we are dealing, in principle, with the most essential needs of each person. This concerns needs that are distributed equally to each, as an intrinsic part of being human. Think of the basic need for food, clothing, housing and such. When one views justice in the sense of granting another person that to which he is actually already entitled – that which he has a right to – then this "needs principle" of justice can represent an assurance for establishing more equality. On the condition, of course, that we are addressing the intrinsic basic needs, those that are really necessary for every dignified existence.

The enterprise versus the state

Especially among captains of industry, the impossibility of realizing both of these principles of justice in the economy is quickly asserted. To strive for both "*to each according to his merits*" and "*to each according to his needs*" would be doomed to short-circuit – if only because the *merits* principle intrinsically produces inequality while the *needs* principle produces equality. In Chapter 3, we already came up against the eternal tension between equality and inequality. Think of actual extreme inequalities within capitalism – in spite of the hypothetical equality of all human beings – or of the extreme equality of communism.

When one insists on taking the merits principle as well as the *needs* principle into account – without burdening the economy with both criteria – then a certain kind of business ethics is bound to let the market economy and the state function as efficiently as possible. Hence, one advocates, respectively, for free economic competition (based on one's merits in the market) and for real political democracy (with a view to the essential needs the state takes on itself). You can argue that, in this way, you are furthering the common good, on the basis of liberal as well as social democratic traditions. From the liberal perspective, the merits principle is based on the free economic market mechanism, while the social democrats focus more on the problem of needs, on the basis of a process of democratic political decision-making.

The common good thus realized, which would amount to the greatest possible degree of justice, also means that we don't simply present human self-interest, with which the principle of profit is often equated, in a negative light. On the contrary: self-interest can be the foundation of the common good, they say. When self-interest does not degenerate into dystopia, as is the case today, it can evoke ethical qualities such as solidarity and compassion. Self-interest and the common good complement one another, just like two buttresses that support the vault in a cathedral. For that reason, both are best co-ordinated in a mixed market economy. This will guarantee the adequate combination of the question of production (efficiency) with the fulfilment of basic needs. As Hobbes pointed out, we need the power of a government to keep the private exercise of power in the national community within the boundaries of the common good.

Efficiency versus equity

At first sight, this mixed economy looks like a logical way out of the tension between the economy and ethics or justice, or the tension between inequality and equality. However, the following question remains (and we already bumped into it in Chapter 3): does this "partition of the estate" between (economic) efficiency and (democratic) equity – in other words, between economics and ethics – remain justified in our time? For the most important implication of the merits principle that is central to the economy is not only that it promotes inequality, but also that it stimulates economic growth and progress, as expressed by the Gross National Product. This is the opposite of the needs principle, which, because it does not stimulate economic performance, has an inhibitory effect on that growth. And thus, at first sight, it seems that it fits with a concept such as Gross National Happiness (think of Peter Van Rompuy's interpretation). But in recent years, it is precisely at the level of economic progress that we witness serious dystopian side-effects. One becomes all too aware of the limits to growth and the limits of progress. That is why people clearly argue that, in the growth of the economy, we have to refocus, from the growth of quantity to the development of quality, lest we undermine ourselves. One must relinquish the old idea of growth, which leads to an unequal gap with our six living worlds, with their respective victims. This view, however, is at odds with the policies that many Western countries continue to adhere to. Here, the growth of Gross National Product prevails over Gross National Happiness. A market that is not restricted by the government ought to realize this growth autonomously. Today's problems are then shifted onto victims such as the environment, the Third and Fourth Worlds, and the quality of our relationships with others at work. Today, people are asking how all this makes any sense.

The shared economy versus the economy of meaningfulness

The limits of growth therefore force us to ask whether, at the economic level, the exclusive merits principle is still sufficient, let alone acceptable. "Yet our doctrinaire approach to the economic system insists that there are only two sides to this economy – the market and government intervention. This willfully neglects the human dimension and is surely a reason why many enterprises neglect the human side of investment" (Shaughnessy, 2015, 305).

It is here that we see the re-emergence of the ethical expansion of the economy, as we discussed in Chapter 3. People stop putting the ethics of merits, which is linked to inequality, at the centre of the economy. Intrinsic basic needs, which are similar for everyone, become just as important, so that we are called upon to share. Solidarity and compassion have thus come to take their place at the heart of the economy. The tension between people's inequality and equality is transcended by putting the equality of people at the centre, as we will see below with Levinas.

So, instead of an economy that is based solely on merit, the *Sharing Economy* that we outlined earlier, for example, comes to the fore: car pooling, sharing one's home through *Airbnb*, local exchange trading systems, shops where you can (learn how to) repair your things (*repair cafés*), free sources of information to which you yourself can contribute (such as *Wikipedia*), *coworking spaces*, where you share overhead costs with others, and so on. In each case, it concerns economic initiatives that, at first sight at least, appear to give intrinsic basic needs the same priority as the need for profit.

It is remarkable that we have a similar development in education, culture and healthcare. In this, it is not just the needs principle that plays a role; often (unfortunately), the merit (profit) principle imposes itself. Both the business model in these sectors and the transition model of, among others, the sharing economy will have to keep justifying themselves, whether, in addition to profit (the merit principle), they also effectively benefit human beings as much as possible (the needs principle). That is why, in Chapter 5, we advocated the regular evaluation of the sharing economy from the perspective of the social economy. Like the public commons, the sharing economy is situated on the bridge between the private and the public sector, so that both the merits principle and the needs principle can be manifested in it.

At first sight, an ethical expansion of the economy is stimulated by the digital disruption our economy is experiencing today (Mason, 2016). It concerns the radical (disruptive) influence of new (information) technologies on the market. Think of the reaction of the hotel sector to *Airbnb*, or the fact that we no longer publish encyclopaedias owing to the rise of *Wikipedia*. Every person becomes a potential disruptor via his Internet connections. As a result, at first sight, it looks like democracy will also get its chance to become more efficient. Networks of small-scale enterprises will then replace the old, often undemocratic, top-down structure of large, regimented companies and governments. Decades ago, Apple adopted this disruptive thinking its approach: "People who are crazy enough to think they can change the world are the ones who do." In this way, starting from a potential trust, each of us could assume our responsibility. This could happen, instead of depending on hierarchical companies and the state, in spite of our labour or vote (Kenis, 2012). Thus, through the sharing economy, the dream of a new economic format for the fulfilment of our needs – among others, for housing and mobility – emerges. This would be great if the Gross National Product did not increase unilaterally. Gross National Happiness could increase as well, if we could see the fulfilment of our needs having a smaller impact on our living environments. If, for example, the environment could suffer less, workers could participate more, the Third and Fourth Worlds could combat victimization, and the world of finance could once again be more of a means for man than an end. Last but not least, the idea of sharing in the economy could recall the idea of meaningfulness in economic activity.

It is therefore important, with the transition in the economy, to assess the sharing economy not only against the social economy, but also against the *purpose economy* we discussed at the beginning of this book. In his 2014 book *The Purpose Economy*, Aaron Hurst explains how, following the agrarian, the industrial and the knowledge economy, we have indeed arrived at the economy of meaningfulness.[84] People are looking for meaningfulness in the economy. This is only possible if they can grow on a personal level, can establish meaningful relationships with others, and can at the same time contribute to the larger whole.[85] Here we hear an echo of the three steps that were prominent in Paul Ricœur's philosophy of responsibility: to find myself as a subject, opposite to the other and within the institutions. Kees Klomp (2016) argues that the economy of meaningfulness is primarily about inspiring people by affirming them in their humanity. Ricœur called this *the confirmation of being*. For Klomp, this is only possible when, as a human being, you mean something on the individual, relational and ecological level. When the economy does not produce meaningfulness, young people from the present generation no longer commit themselves to it. Hurst (2014, 7) summarizes the purpose economy as a "call to action for all of us working towards an economy that serves people and the planet". He proves empirically that, just as the knowledge economy increasingly determined the entire economy, this now appears increasingly to be the case with the purpose economy: "The Purpose Economy impacts all the sectors in the broader economy, like the Information Economy has done" (2014, 41).

Justice can thus become righteousness. In righteousness, justice starts from a point of discovered meaningfulness. A crucial question that transcends the scope of this book is the question of whether the current technological revolution that lurks behind the shared

---

84 Compare this with Geert Noels' *Econoshock* (2008). This book also fits seamlessly with the paradigm of the economy of meaningfulness.

85 See also Bailey (2016).

economy, or behind post-capitalism in general, is threatening meaningfulness. We often hear that the necessary economic disruption depends on daring and trust. Can we still speak of daring and trust when technology steers us away from meaningfulness? The *Economy of Communion* proves particularly well how, with the transition of our economy, meaningfulness behind any enterprise is a vital stepping-stone to establishing justice and responsibility in an authentic way. The *Economy of Communion* is at work in around 700 companies all over the world. Though it emerged from a Christian background, its outlook has now become actively pluralistic. These companies combine the principles of a free market with an extremely consistent philosophy of responsibility. Their profits are systematically distributed to sustainable investment in the enterprise itself, the creation of meaningful employment and the provision of help to those in need.[86]

In general, we can say that, while in the *shared economy* the focus is still on the individual, we see happiness emerge through a focus on our fellow man and nature, in the *social economy*, the *economy of meaningfulness* and the *economy of communion*, and this in the line of Ricœur and Levinas. Thus, starting from *social economy*, passing through the *purpose economy*, all the way to the *economy of communion*, justice is, increasingly, becoming *righteousness*.

Economic Justice Inspired by Levinas

From egology to otherness

In the previous chapter, we explored Paul Ricœur's personalist philosophical foundation of responsibility, apart from a theistic or atheistic framework. We will now engage with the philosophy of Emmanuel Levinas in our discussion.[87] As a Jewish philosopher, Levinas starts from the concept of justice as well, but he bases this on the way justice is developed in the Torah, that is, as righteousness. Levinas confronts righteousness with Western philosophy. He argues that, since

---

86 http://www.edc-online.org/en/

87 In a previous work (1989) which I co-authored with Wim Thys and Antoon Vandevelde, Thys developed an introduction to Levinas's philosophy of responsibility, which I am building on here.

modernity, Western philosophy and its theories of justice (think of Hobbes) have been characterized by a form of *egology* (Edmund Husserl's "science of the ego"), because they were focused on liberal freedom, self-interest or the principle of merit. As a result, attention to victims, such as the poor or the environment, was relegated to the background. As Levinas sees it, justice became more and more "in-different" instead of "right-eous". In contrast to income distribution, the essential differences between people are increasingly erased. A philosophy of indifference has emerged. People are only judged by what they have in common. Our wonder about the actual *other-ness* of the other evaporates. It was this egology that was expressed in the first presupposition of the economy. As a result, nature, labour and technology are becoming indifferent data through which man indulges his self-interest.

However, in his specific theory of justice, Levinas emphasizes difference – *otherness* (or "alterity", from the French "altérité") – over indifference. According to Levinas, we can find the roots of the philosophy of indifference in Western metaphysics, in which ontology (the thinking about everything that is) reduces all of reality to *being*, and all the elements of this reality (nature, workers, etc.) to *beings* as well. Whether it's about objects, nature or God, Western philosophy itself became an ontology: the reduction of the other to the same. This is how otherness was reduced to identity. It is the exception when otherness is developed, for example, in the specificity of nature or transcendence, or in the way Descartes treats infinity. Kant also speaks of a "reality behind reality" that appears to us, and urges us to respect our fellow man, instead of subjecting him to the power of the ego. Although Martin Buber also distinguishes between the "I–thou" and the "I–it" relationships, Levinas felt that he does not go far enough in the recognition of otherness. Only fundamental respect for otherness and differentiation can fundamentally release people from an objectifying levelling. It is this levelling that characterized the domains of economic dystopia that we discussed earlier, with their respective victims: the worker who is crushed by relentless standardized performance metrics; the poor created as a result of the degradation of human development and reduction of happiness to the Gross National Product; environmental degradation arising from the levelling of economic logic. In summarizing this objectifying levelling, Levinas refers to the "il-y-a".

In order to liberate himself from this, man needs to develop a sustaining selfhood. Levinas refers to a self-identification, or interiority, that expresses an otherness. It is striking that Levinas does not consider this emergence of man's selfhood so much in, say, pleasure or knowledge, but in the economic sphere. He views living and shelter as the beginning of the economy, and sees labour as its completion. From the intimacy of the home, the encounter with the Other becomes possible, but it is also labour that enables humans to get a grip on the things around them.

From self-interest towards the face of the other

Fundamentally, however, man is interested in himself. This manifests itself in the second presupposition of the economy, the presupposition of individuality. When only this self-interest plays a role regarding the other human being, the world or nature, not only will you never reach the actual truth of the other but you will fail to reach your own truth. It becomes necessary to shift from the discovery of the other to letting the face of the other reveal itself in full. For Levinas, the power of the self-searching and self-discovering individual is symbolized in war. In the economy, one speaks of competition. As we saw with Hobbes and Girard, the living together of people turns into a permanent civil war. One exploits the Other to realize one's own freedom, as a result of which the originality of the other human being disappears into nothingness. The Other degenerates into an object. Thus, in the economy, when you disregard the other person, you threaten to render him into a mere instrument. In the philosophy of contract, the contract becomes the solution for the clash of one man's egoism with the egoism of the other. In this arrangement, everybody is prepared to relinquish some freedom, as we observed in the compromise between the principles of *merits* and of *needs* in business ethics. For instance, you are willing to pay taxes to the state in exchange for order. In such a contract, as we learned from Rousseau in the previous chapter, we are also confronted with the tension between *freedom* (as with the principle of merits) and *order* (as with the principle of needs). According to Levinas, living together is thus reduced to a kind of technique of social equilibrium which, as we've seen, attempts to create harmony between forces that are battling each other. The fundamental category behind the contract, however, is self-interest. In fact, the threat of the violence of war is shrouded by a kind of humanism of the "I" that displaces the violence by creating victims in society, as we saw with Girard.

From desire to longing

According to Levinas, the compromise solution of the philosophers of contract can only be transcended by once again looking to the experience that characterizes every origin of coexistence: the face-to-face encounter. In our initial encounters, long before we decide we need a contract, we realize that the Other is more than what we might desire from him, as Girard puts it. Think of people who fall in love with each other and only later decide they need a contract. But today's economy is based on desire. That is why scarcity, the third presupposition of the economy, is created over and over again (think of advertising). Paul Ricœur argued that because I want to become myself and also want to develop my individual power, I conclude a contract with the other. According to Levinas, this is characteristic of the desire that is focused on a world that is already there for me. This is the original form of the self-identification which we discussed, and which, according to Levinas, amounts to egoism, selfishness. At this stage of Levinas's reasoning, we recognize the *fear*, and the desire that flows from it, whereby we – with help from Hobbes, Girard and others – explained the origins of a modern economy that leads to dystopia.

It is, however, fundamentally true for Levinas that, in the encounter between people, *longing* can emerge just as well. We're dealing here with an economy in transition. Here, the *recognition of the other* (alterity) is central. The other isn't brought into the world of the ego just like that. On the contrary: in longing, the ego opens itself to the Other. My sovereign self-identification is embarrassed. Levinas calls this manifestation of the other "the revelation of the naked face". As a result, the other is always more than and different from what he shows from within my own fear and desire. It is here that Levinas finds the foundation of what he rightly calls "a new humanism". For him, this is the humanism of our infinite responsibility for the fate of the other. Classical economic relationships, as we've seen, presuppose infinite *needs* based upon desire, instead of infinite *responsibility*. As a result, the other person is infinitely exploited instead of infinitely respected.

From social morality to authentic ethics

Levinas's humanism, based on respecting the other in his otherness ('alterity'), is the foundation for a more intensive form of justice than the classical compromise between the principles of merits and of needs. Levinas calls this more radical form of justice, one we have come to on the basis of the economic realty, "righteousness". With this, you *respect* the other in his inalienable freedom. Instead of merely balancing freedom (the market), and the principle of merits, with order (the state) or the principle of needs, you *receive* the other as he is. In terms of the fourth presupposition of the economy, labour then isn't just a means in the service of profit, but also an end in itself, with an eye on respect for the worker. According to Levinas, the gap created by the economy with its victims (from the person with burn-out, the poor, the refugee, all the way to the pillage of nature) assumes a different light: "The transcendence of the face is at the same time its absence from the world it enters, the exiling of a being, his condition of being stranger, destitute, or proletarian" (2012, 75).

Although Levinas, as a Jewish philosopher, develops this new interpretation of justice within the context of a righteousness that draws on the Torah, he approaches the self-revelation of the other within the context of the original manifestation of ethics. The distinction between atheistic and theistic philosophers of responsibility that we described earlier is thus transcended in an actively pluralistic manner. Levinas names this by discussing what he calls "authentic ethics". This also transcends the social morality that only serves the humanism of the ego. In this, the other is indeed often viewed as a mere means. Through the individuality of the other, my economic complacency is challenged and labelled self-betrayal.

From parity to equality

The authentic ethics that Levinas posits, therefore, does not depart from the anxious, desiring ego, but from the fact that in our society the weak Others (people with burn-out, the poor among us and far away, nature, etc.) are reduced as victims instead of being respected as the starting-point or centre of our (economic) practices. That is why otherness becomes the primary value of ethics. This is the reverse of the primacy of parity upon which Hobbes based his treatment of fear and desire as the foundations of the economy. In fact, the fifth presupposition of the economy was based on this: to express everything in terms of the same or a similar measure, to wit, utility. There is no role for the qualitative difference between meaningless and meaningful goods and services, for example. In Levinas's vision of justice, parity evolves into equivalence, countering the tendency to classify concrete economic transition projects as a kind of new collectivism à la Marx.

Central to this righteousness mode of justice is what Levinas calls goodness. It is an expression of what we have called (Christian) mercy or (Buddhist) compassion. Crucial to this goodness (as we also saw with the Great Vehicle of Buddhism) is that responsibility for concrete fellow humans (by way of the face) confronts us with the presence of third parties. There is not only my own world and that of the concrete Other. There is also the South or the Fourth World of the poor. According to Levinas, in the face of the Other, eventually the whole world looks at me. In this sense, Levinas's I–you relationship transcends the I–thou relationship of Buber, which probably came across as too private.

From goodness to universal responsibility

As we've seen, the presuppositions of our free-market economy are due for a rephrasing, or transition. When responsibility comes first within the economic presuppositions, it is no longer necessary for the market economy to refer exclusively to politics – that is, if we want something to happen at the level recognizing the essential needs of man and nature, or preventing excessive inequalities. In terms of the sixth presupposition of the economy, then, the market is no longer the moulding, through prices, of irresponsibility into an officially accepted institution. Incorporating responsibility into the economy enables us to combine the principle of merit with the principle of needs within the economy itself. Of course, the government can still intervene to lend its support. However, in Levinas's approach, our transitioning economy can *itself* assume responsibility for the victims that our economic activity creates. In terms that remind us of Paul Ricœur's philosophy of responsibility, Levinas states: "In the measure that the face of the other relates us with the third party, the metaphysical relation of the I with the other moves into the form of the We, aspires to a State, institutions, laws, which are the source of universality" (2012, 300). Thus, the idea of mankind is the foundational category by which this universal responsibility is constructed. The idea of a concrete economic utopia developed in this book, along the lines of the thinking of Levinas, therefore amounts to the utopia of a universal brotherhood emerging from a variety of concrete forms of this *responsibility towards the other*.

Although we will return shortly to the new perspective on money and prices that results from this, we can, as a stepping-stone, start by looking at Levinas's original responsibility-focused view of money. According to Levinas, money is mainly meant to enable an easy exchange of goods and services. It becomes possible to recognize the other human being who offers these goods and services, instead of acquiring them by means of violence. Of course, you might say that money equalizes or objectifies the priceless value of the human labour that is hidden within these commodities and services without acknowledging it intrinsically. This is also a potential criticism of the attempt at gauging human happiness with a measuring method such as Gross National Happiness (Levinas's "negative objectivity"). Is money then still the perfect means of an individualistic economy through which the service or labour of man is equated with objects that can be paid in the shape of wages, and whereby the labour that is hidden in these objects is forgotten (Levinas, 1986)? Righteousness, however, makes it possible for money to serve more than an ego-centred economy. In addition to self-interest, disinterest is also possible. Active elimination of self-interest enables us, according to Levinas, to point out the importance of giving (money) as a specific relationship with the other, whom we recognize in his individuality. When money is given away, we are no longer beset by a negative objectivity that neglects the intrinsic value of human labour. We're concerned here with a positive objectivity that doesn't simply identify value in a monetary way, but also enables differentiation, for instance, by being generous with the poor on specific occasions – generous with your money. Economists such as Stefan Zamagni and Luigino

Bruni make this concrete by assigning a central place to sharing in the *Economy of Communion* in which they operate. Not just with regard to shareholders and employees, but also in the social projects that an entrepreneur wishes to promote. It's a kind of *Gift Economy*, or a literal form of the *Sharing Economy*.[88]

A Responsible Economy

How shall we amend the presuppositions of the present economy that we mentioned at the beginning of this chapter? Which points of departure do we need to develop if we want to prevent our economy from establishing dystopia? But also: which basic principles are necessary to avoid ending up in a naive utopia? It is clear that the conclusion of this book will not be that we all need to move together towards an economy like Bhutan, be it via the social economy, the purpose economy or the economy of communion. In the first place, just as *meaningfulness* is always a challenge or an invitation that becomes problematic when you impose it, so too are the alternatives outlined in this book. The *Social Economy*, the *Purpose Economy* and the *Economy of Communion* can never be an end in themselves. They constitute a friendly but unambiguous appeal for every economic endeavour on this earth. It is up to the reader, society and, above all, coming generations to judge whether companies like Trader Joe's, DSW (Designer Shoe Warehouse), REI and local credit unions have succeeded in bringing about concrete changes that are inspired by the paradigm of responsibility. Let us list the starting points and see how they are working out in practice today.

Responsible, as in Responsible Economics

First of all, in the economy, we can no longer be indifferent to data such as nature, labour, technology and, last but not least, our so-called infinite needs. We discover that this cluster of data happens to contain the most important factors that cause the economy to degenerate into dystopia. Starting with the philosophers, and practices, of responsibility, we can transform this cluster of data into a *cluster of*

---

88 See also Leonard (2014).

responsibility. Thus, it concerns a series of data which you can no longer simply view as exogenous (derived externally), but for which you assume responsibility. In Levinas's thinking, you arrive at the consciousness of its otherness (its *alterity*). The objectifying levelling disappears.

There is thus more and more talk of what one calls *Responsible Economics*, or a responsible economy.[89] With regard to (among other things) the ecosystem, labour, technology, as well as our infinite needs, one no longer escapes one's responsibility. The worldwide CSR (Corporate Social Responsibility) approach in the economy also illustrates this abundantly.[90] Our sense of responsibility focuses not only on profits, but also on the social (that is, people), and on the ecosystem (the planet).[91] The Organization for Economic Co-operation and Development (OECD) *guidelines* contain concrete recommendations to make this economic responsibility a reality. Indeed, rich countries bear a special responsibility, given their power and technological advantage.

Thus, the etymological meaning of the word "economy" has been reinstated, to wit: "oikonomia" (*oikos*: house, and *nomos*: rule), the totality of rules that guarantee the "good governance of a household". The term "good" here is not separate from the philosophy of responsibility. As we learned earlier, Aristotle had already distinguished the term "oikonomia" from what he called "chrematistics" (the art of acquiring riches). Instead of an economy that is responsible towards our world or globe, a globalized chrematistics has arisen. If only for the living world of the environment, the emergence of a cluster of responsibility is a blessing.

Inter-human, as in the Social Economy

A result of this cluster of responsibility, which is getting attention all over the world now, is that there is a greater emphasis on the inter-personal, the *inter-human*, than on individualism. As Levinas pointed out, one arrives at the genuine truth of the Other. For this,

89 See also Opdebeeck (2012, 2013a).

90 See also Opdebeeck (2013b).

91 See also Opdebeeck (2011b).

the transition from self-discovery of the other to allowing the face of the other to reveal itself is essential. The satisfaction of fundamental human needs – for respect and self-development – depends primarily on the quality of the inter-human relationships concerned. Only by way of a qualitatively rich personal relationship with the other do you encounter human needs at a deeper level. Whereas in the present economy, competition is steadily increased, the satisfaction of essential human needs demands co-operation and solidarity.

The *Social Economy* discussed above attempts to convert this into practice. As we have argued, this is more evident among co-operatives than in what we often see happening in the *Sharing* (or *Collaborative*[92]) *Economy*. While the prevailing paradigm pays too much attention to the relationship between man and object, in the social economy one attaches essential importance to the other. From this point of view of inter-human relationship, you thus attack the gap between you and the second world (that is, the other). Here, the other can be a colleague or client, a patient, the poor, a foreigner, the disabled, and so on.

Enough, as in the Circular Economy

Subsequently, the choice for a responsible attitude in economics puts the infinitude of human needs and desire in question. It is important to recommend a limit, a *finitude*, to human needs, if only for the sake of yet another element of the aforementioned cluster of responsibility, to wit, the environment. Levinas talks about a desire that turns into a longing in which the other is acknowledged as another, and you open yourself to the Other. You ignore mimetic desire. Thus, we will talk about *an economy of enough*, rather than our dystopian economy of dissatisfaction.

This is reflected in what we call a *Circular Economy*. Central to a circular economy is the prevention of the exhaustion of scarce resources, the recycling of waste, and the use of energy sources such as the wind and the sun. The economist Kenneth Boulding might be considered the spiritual father of this economic paradigm. He had already talked about the economy of *Spaceship Earth* in 1966.[93] The

---

92 See also Opdebeeck (2010a).

93 http://dieoff.org/page160.htm

already mentioned report to the Club of Rome, *The Limits to Growth* (1972), put the necessity of a circular economy on the political agenda for the first time. Actual applications include, among others, *Cradle-to-Cradle* projects, in which one produces on the basis of components that can be reused after their cycle of life has run out. A more radical form of a circular economy is what one calls an *Economy of Frugality* (Opdebeeck, 2008). Here, far more than in a circular economy, moderation, temperance, is paramount. Frugality comes from the Latin word *frux*, fruit. One doesn't cultivate frugality in the economy out of masochism, but in view of the fertility that manifests itself in happiness. Here, we may point to E. F. Schumacher as the spiritual father.[94]

A result of this third principle is that it enables us to view the gap between the First and the Third World (the South) from the perspective of a fairer distribution (on the basis of a fertile point of sufficiency for the West), rather than from the perspective of the average Westerner who can never get enough. This puts the gap with the South in a different perspective.

Balanced, as in Happiness Economics

The stated distinction in the economy between the means (such as labour or technology) and the ends that must be achieved (profit, for example) is criticized because this distinction detracts from our respect for the other. For in terms of Levinas, you desire to respect the other in his inalienable freedom. To receive the other as he is cannot be reconciled with using him or her as a means towards an end. On the contrary, in a sensible way, *means and ends* have to be balanced *relative to each other* in view of man's happiness.[95]

In the *Happiness Economy*, we see that certain aspects of this view have been developed with, among others, Richard Layard as a pioneering thinker and *Gross National Happiness* as an application. Money is then a means and not an end. Through adapted forms of technology that do not undermine human happiness, you are given the chance not to regard machines as merely a means with a

---

94 See also Opdebeeck (2013b).

95 See also Opdebeeck (2015).

view to achieving maximum efficiency. When labour as a means is too drastically reduced in favour of capital, you will feel the need to re-emphasize the neglected value of qualitatively rich, rewarding labour as its own end. If only for employment in the Fourth World (the poor among us), we see a hopeful change.

Authentic, as in the Purpose Economy

A fifth offshoot of the transition in the economy is the fact that the principle of rationality, according to which the economic subject takes those decisions that maximize utility, is put in perspective (Wilkinson, 2007). In light of the cluster of responsibility and, among others, Maslow's hierarchy of needs, the emphasis has shifted towards the *more authentic needs* of man. Think of the need for respect and self-development that we discussed earlier.

It is this emphasis on authenticity that is also central to the *Purpose Economy* in which one embarks upon the search for meaning. Not just through personal achievements, but at least as much through meaningful contacts with others and contributions to the *bonum commune*, the common good.[96] Thus, economic growth is focused not so much on the further increase of the consumption of material goods, but much more on services that are useful for the ethical and cultural enhancement of living standards or happiness.

However, such an alternative cannot be easily realized in a society in which the population is stimulated every day to possess and/or consume ever more material goods. This is due to the impact of a predominantly materialist ethical foundation that can block the human drive to reach a higher level in the hierarchy of needs, let alone to be receptive to the other-*ness* of the other, in line with the authentic ethics of Levinas. However, when we don't obscure man's authentic needs (through a maximization of utility that can be expressed in terms of money), we soon stop jumping to the conclusion that labour is useless. Instead, we emphasize the fact that labour is important for human development. One shifts the focus in the economy from the real to the financial sphere. Through ethical banking, one tries to

---

96 See also Opdebeeck (2010b).

prevent the constant increase of the aforementioned gap between real and financial worlds.

Meaningful, as in the Economy of Communion

Finally, from the perspective of responsibility, an ethically expanded economy will adopt a different attitude towards the price presupposition of the prevailing economy. This assumption makes it all too easy for individual utility seekers to co-ordinate their respective preferences. However, it is not because something or someone doesn't yield an immediate utility that it is therefore without value or needs to be priced through some method of assessment.

By proposing that things can only be *partially expressed in money*, we can avoid reducing values that cannot be expressed in money to a common denominator of "price". We don't just reduce elderly people to a cost. The same goes for the daily labour of a spouse at home, for nature, and for human life in general. According to Levinas, from such concrete invitations to assume responsibility, a universal brotherhood emerges. You do not merely propose so-called solutions such as an affordable retirement home, potential wages for homemakers, or cost–benefit analyses.

In all of this, you stop reasoning in terms of pure prices in the service of your self-interest. On the contrary: as in the worldwide *Economy of Communion*, in line with Levinas, the focus is on generous sharing.[97] As has been shown, the profits of an enterprise of the Economy of Communion flow not only to sustainable investments, but also to meaningful work and concrete support for those who are on the edge of society, on whom it is hard to simply put a price.

97 See also Opdebeeck (2011c).

7. Conclusion

It is utopian to present the economy as a place where human happiness is as paramount as profit. That is the opinion of many who might pick up this book. This truism, analogous to the argument that Gross National Happiness is utopian, is, however, confronted by the actual situation of our economy today. Our globalized society, with its Gross National Product, turns out to be a dystopia. Our globe has indeed become a place where it is no longer that pleasant to live. From burnt-out people at the workplace, via the gap with the Southern Hemisphere, to our threatened environment: there is not much left of the utopia of the free market. The aim for at least the last fifty years, since the Club of Rome, to transform it into a *sustainable* economy is failing.

The traditional tension between the economy and ethics thus translates into an untenable tension. On the one hand, you have the raw reality of the rational market economy that is gaining ground everywhere since the disappearance of communism. On the other, you're not allowed to dream of a reasonable *happiness* economy in which human beings are paramount. Fortunately, today we are rediscovering justice as a crucial ethical concept. Without justice, our society and our economy will perish. At the same time, however, we realize that neither the government-guaranteed economic order nor social contracts based on justice suffice. Because we give ever more priority to our individual freedom, it is clear that, in order to guarantee justice, but also to stop fear and dystopia, we need to take responsibility. This is a highly necessary completion of the difficult synthesis between order and freedom. It is in this way that, according to Levinas, justice becomes righteousness. Not, as with a utopia, to make man's happiness a reality in the future, or at a specific location, but here and now, and all over the world. In a dialectical manner, a realistic synthesis of utopia and dystopia has come about.

On the occasion of the 500th anniversary of the publication of Thomas More's *Utopia*, we can express this through a new concept: *uglobia*. In "uglobia", the "u" refers to "*eu*", the Greek stem for happiness. Confusion with the Greek stem "*ou*", which evokes the connotation of "utopia" as "impossible", can thus gradually disappear with the newly coined word uglobia. Uglobia is concerned with the transition of our globalized society here and now, in such a way that the Gross National Product serves Gross National Happiness. Only in this way can we avoid the bad luck of our unequal world. The net happiness of as many people as possible on our globe (uglobia) is now paramount, not that of a minority in a few places. In this sense, uglobia isn't just another view of utopia, but also another perspective on globalization, one that transcends the polarization between contemporary pessimistic versus optimistic economists such as Nouriel Roubini (2011) and Joseph Stiglitz (2015).

I initially launched *uglobia* as a term for another vision of utopian thinking and globalization on 6 May 2006, at an international conference in Siena devoted to "Ethical Choices in Society, the Economy and the Environment" (Opdebeeck, 2007). The conference was sponsored by the oldest bank in the world, the Banca Monte dei Paschi di Siena, originally the Monte di Pietà, the "Mountain of Mercy". This bank was founded in 1472 to, among other things, protect the needy from usury interests. Siena is also home to one of the earliest hospitals that also took care of the poor: Santa Maria della Scala, where the 2006 conference took place. Each time, we are confronted here by metaphors for meaningful institutions, whether economic or not, that are focused on the happiness of the human being and the common good that is the central concern of this book.

Focusing on the economy in combination with happiness and the common good requires us to re-study scarcity, the foundation of our economy. As a result, an extra dimension emerges that is important if we hope to give uglobia a chance. For an unrestrained desire for economic growth based on scarcity confronts us with the forgotten meaningfulness behind the economic. The desire for ever more economic growth appears, in fact, to emerge from the desire to give meaningfulness to our fear, our suffering, our hope, our longing and our happiness. This creates economic utopia and dystopia. Especially by comparing ourselves with others, we produce and shop ever more. As a result, we create varieties of scarcity we want to struggle against. Think of the shortage of decent human workplaces, the shortage of resources for the poor here and around the world, and the lack of diversity in the environment. Economics as the desire to ban material scarcity from the world therefore invites us to work out an economy that rediscovers the sense of warding off the scarcity of what is most dear to us in our living worlds.

Just as uglobia transcends the tension between utopia and dystopia, trust can bridge the tension between suffering and happiness. This is something that we no longer need to hear only from religion, but that we can determine just as well on the basis of clinical psychological research. Trust appears to work like lubricating oil when we responsibly hoist the sails of our globalized economic ship. Thus, we stop being dependent on sacrifices to various gods like money and power, with their well-known effects, such as burnout, poverty and environmental crisis. Both the atheist and the believer appeal to us to take responsibility effectively, on the basis of one or the other form of trust. This trust comes about actively pluralistic in several ways. For example, it can happen by way of the *thaumasia* (the philosopher's wonder), by way of the mystical consolation like that of Eckhart, or by way of the loving friendliness of the Buddha. A society that is ravaged by market and religious fundamentalism should no longer pronounce vetoes against sources of inspiration for trust in a concrete uglobia that transcends the dystopia of the market and of terrorism. The essence of what we mean by trust, to wit, the belief that someone or something can be trusted, leads us to the insight that responsibility emerges from equality. Compassion as an authentic expression of responsibility starts from this equality, for people, but also for the environment.

Today, we recognize the results of this uglobia all over the world. We hear a lot about Responsible Economics, Happiness Economics, Circular Economics, the Economy of Frugality, the Collaborative Economy, the Sharing Economy and the Gift Economy. In this book, we have mainly made a plea for economic practices as elaborated in the Social Economy, the Purpose Economy and the Economy of Communion. Time and again, these are manifestations of an economic transition that, to a greater or lesser degree, no longer focuses exclusively on principles such as scarcity, individualism or utility. Responsibility, the interpersonal and authenticity are at least as central. Each time, they are concrete challenges that are pertinent responses to the tension between utopia and dystopia. It is not a matter of fanatically reversing all economic activity in our globalized society in the direction of an economy of meaningfulness. But the unmistakably obvious challenge that the alternatives represent has something of an appealing urgency. We are no longer obliged to organize our economy around deadly fear or naive hope. A look at the face of past, present and future generations is enough to make resolute work of giving meaningfulness to the economy.

Afterword by Ludo Abicht[98]

The concept of "happiness": you can start with an extremely individual dream of happiness, such as that of a homeless person in San Francisco, and arrive at a socio-economic experiment, such as the present kingdom of Bhutan, which the homeless person may never even have heard of. Or you can start with a relatively successful co-operative enterprise, such as Mondragon in Catalonia, and arrive at the daydreams of illiterate and exploited factory girls in Bangladesh. From the individual to the universal and back. Nobody will deny that these daydreams cannot possibly be detached from the gratification of the material needs of citizens and society; while it is true that man does not live on bread alone, he cannot, however, survive without that bread. So it is not surprising that the tensions between ethics, the teaching of the good (happy) life and the economy – and generally between utopia and dystopia – keep coming up in anyone's search for meaningfulness in our personal and public (economic) life.

In this book, Hendrik Opdebeeck explores the boundaries of the dominant economy and, with a number of fellow economists and philosophers, arrives at the conclusion that it is high time that we relinquish the still-praised model of productivity in order to invent and develop a new economic paradigm. A model in which (to quote the text of *The Acts of the Apostles*, as well as the socialists later) "everybody truly receives according to his needs". With the crucial nuance that in our culture, those "needs" comprise much more than the gratification of our material needs. Of course, that is where it starts, but that is not where it ought to end. In California, there is a retail chain for home, kitchen and bathroom appliances with the catchy name "Bed, Bath & Beyond". In the discussions about a possible, that is to say *achievable*,

---

[98] Ludo Abicht teaches philosophy at PARTS (Brussels). Previously he taught philosophy and cultural history at Antioch College and the University of California, Berkeley.

concrete utopian economy, we are in fact talking about this "beyond", circumstances that go far beyond the needs for food, rest and hygiene. An economy that takes account of the struggle against alienation and instrumentalization in the name of profit. In the pre-capitalist stage of our economy, tools, such as hammers and sickles, were nothing more than extensions in the service of humans who, in employing these tools, were able to create a better life for themselves and their offspring. In the industrialized world, man, according to Marx, was rather turned into an extension of the machine, whether it concerns a simple spinning mill or a fully automated, digitalized factory, of which Charlie Chaplin's *Modern Times* already sketched a painfully accurate caricature in 1936.

Opdebeeck critically analyses the many proposals that are circulating today that deal with models for turning the economy of the future to the service of (ever broader and deeper) human needs. He comes to the conclusion that none of them is without a problem or can guarantee complete success, from ethical banking and the Sharing Economy to the various forms of the "Economy of Happiness". For in Bhutan as well, it appears that the (utopian) success of material production brings about the danger of a (dystopian) loss of compassion and solidarity. This excellently informed book thus provokes us to think further, to be realistically anchored in the tangible and measurable facts, on the basis of that which has been invented and tested previously, but to be sufficiently free-thinking. The important mission of this book is to pursue the development of a future international commonwealth in which inequality will be diminished to the point where we can create space for the greatest possible development of all people, starting with the billions of fellow human beings who are still falling overboard.

Bibliography

Abicht, L. and H. Opdebeeck (2015), *The Point of Philosophy* (Oxford/Brussels: Peter Lang).

Achterhuis, H. (1988), *Het rijk van de schaarste* (Baarn: Ambo).

Achterhuis, H. (1998), *De Erfenis Van de Utopie* (Baarn: Ambo).

Achterhuis, H. (2006), *Utopie* (Baarn: Ambo).

Achterhuis, H. (2010), *De utopie van de vrije markt* (Rotterdam: Lemniscaat).

Amato, J. (2002), *Mounier and Maritain: A French Catholic Understanding of the Modern World* (Ypsilanti: Sapientia).

Amin, A. (2009), *The Social Economy, International Perspectives on Economic Solidarity* (London: Zed Books).

Ariely, D., E. Kamenica and D. Prelec (2008), Man's search for meaning: the case of Legos, *Journal of Economic Behavior and Organisation*, 67, pp. 671–7.

Arnsperger, C. (2013), Small is beautiful: but is it responsible? A critical reappraisal of E. F. Schumacher's contribution to ecological economics and political ecology, in H. Opdebeeck (2013), *Responsible Economics, E.F. Schumacher and His Legacy for the 21st Century* (Oxford: Peter Lang), pp. 127–50.

Bailey, C. and A. Madden (2016), What makes work meaningful or meaningless, *MIT Sloan Management Review*, 57(4). ISSN 1532-9194.

Barrez, D. (2014), *Coöperaties, Hoe heroveren we de economie?* (Antwerp: Epo).

Bauwens, M. (2013), *De wereld redden* (Antwerp: Houtekiet).

Becker, M. (2001), *Economie & Ethiek in Dialoog* (Assen: Van Gorcum).

Benkler, Y. (2004), Sharing nicely: on shareable goods and the emergence of sharing as a modality of economic production, *The Yale Law Journal*, 114, pp. 273–358.

Bloch, E. (1967), *Das Prinzip Hoffnung* (Frankfurt am Main: Suhrkamp).

Bloch, E. (1986), *Freiheit und Ordnung, Abriss der Sozialutopien* (Frankfurt am Main: Suhrkamp).

Boey, K. (1993), *Een prijswaardige economie* (Groot-Bijgaarden: Selektief-Infotex).

Borg, M. ter (2003), *Zineconomie. De samenleving van de overtreffende trap* (Schiedam: Scriptum).

Bormans, M. (ed.) (2016), *The World Book of Hope: The Source of Success, Strength and Happiness* (Tielt: Lannoo).

Botsman, R. (2010), *What's Mine Is Yours* (New York: HarperBusiness).

Bouckaert, L. (2005), *Spiritualiteit, Bedrijfsethiek en Ondernemersschap* (Wilrijk: VKW).

Bouckaert, L. (ed.) (2015), *Business, Ethics and Peace* (Bingley: Emerald).

Boudry, M. (2015), *Illusies voor gevorderden* (Antwerp: Polis).

Boone, B. et al. (2016), On the possibility and driving forces of secular stagnation, working paper, UGent.

Buber, M. (1950), *Paths in Utopia* (New York: Syracuse University Press).

Buber, M. (1937), *I and Thou* (London: Continuum).

Cagle, S. (2014), The case against sharing: on access, scarcity, and trust, *Medium.com*, 28 May.

Cayley, D. (2005), *The Rivers North of the Future: The Testament of Ivan Illich* (Toronto: House of Anansi).

Decreus, T. and C. Callewaert (2016), *Dit is morgen* (Berchem: EPO).

De Grauwe, P. (2015), Het milieu is de achillespees van het kapitalisme, *De Standaard Weekblad*, July.

Desmet, M. (2013), *Bruto Nationaal Geluk, Bhutan inspireert de wereld* (Tielt: Lannoo).

De Visscher, J., H. Opdebeeck and J. Van Gerwen (1995), *Het probleem van de grondslagen van de moraal* (Kampen: Kok Agora).

Deweer, D. (2013), The political theory of personalism: Maritain and Mounier on personhood and citizenship, *International Journal of Philosophy and Theology*, 74(2), pp. 108–26.

Dumouchel, D. (1979), L'Ambivalence de la rareté, in J. P. Dupuy, and P. Dumouchel, *L'Enfer des Choses: René Girard et la logique de l'économie* (Paris: Seuil), pp. 137–254.

Dupré, L. (2015), Roger Lenaers en de mythen van het Christendom, *Streven*, Dec., pp. 996–1,003.

Eckhardt, G. and F. Bardhi (2015), The Sharing Economy isn't about sharing at all, *Harvard Business Review*, 28 Jan.

Fragnière, G. (2006), *Hendrik Brugmans, Building Europe by Educating Europeans* (Brussels: Madariaga European Foundation).

Ferry, L. (2006), *Apprendre à vivre* (Paris: Plon).

Ferry, L. (2010), *Learning to Live* (Edinburgh: Canongate).

Frenken, K. (2016), *Deeleconomie onder één noemer*, Inaugurele rede uitgesproken bij de aanvaarding van het ambt van hoogleraar in Innovation Studies aan de faculteit Geowetenschappen (Utrecht: Universiteit Utrecht).

Geurtz, J. (2016), *Addicted to Love: The Path to Self-Acceptance and Happiness in Relations* (Amsterdam: Ambo, Anthos).

Girard, R. (1978), *Des choses cachées depuis la fondation du monde* (Paris : Grasset).

Goudzwaard, B. (1979), *Capitalism and Progress* (Toronto: Wedge Publishing).

Hauttekeete, E. (2009), *Onder de bodhiboom, Het boeddhisme in zijn historische context* (Brussels: Kunchab).

Hill, S. (2015), *Raw Deal. How the "UberEconomy" and Runaway Capitalism Are Screwing American Workers* (New York: St. Martin's Press).

Hobbes, J., *Leviathan*.

Holemans, D. (2015), De ecologische missing link van Piketty. Een ecologische kritiek van Het Kapitaal van de 21ste Eeuw, *Oikos* 73(2), pp. 31–43.

Hügel, F. von (1909, rev. 1923), *The Mystical Element of Religion* (London: Dent).

Hurst, A. (2014), *The Purpose Economy* (Boise: Elevate).

Illich, I. (2014), *De rivieren ten noorden van de toekomst.Laatste gesprekken over religie en samenleving met David Cayley* (Kalmthout: Pelckmans-Klement).

Jackson, T. (2009), *Prosperity without Growth, Economics for a Finite Planet* (London and New York: Earthscan/Routledge).

Jaspers, K. (1949), *Vom Ursprung und Ziel der Geschichte* (Munich: Piper).

Jaspers, K. (1962), *Socrates, Buddha, Confucius, Jesus: The Paradigmatic Individuals* (New York: Harcourt Brace & Co.).

Karlsson, N., G. Loewenstein, and J. McCafferty (2004), The economics of meaning, *Nordic Journal of Political Economy*, 30(1), pp. 61–75.

Kenis, A. and M. Lievens (2016), *De mythe van de groene economie* (Berchem: Epo).

Kenis, A. and M. Lievens (2017), *The Limits of the Green Economy* (London: Routledge).

Klomp, K. (2016), *Handboek Betekenisvol Ondernemen* (Amsterdam: Atlas-Contact).

Kołakowski, L. (2001), *Religion: If There Is No God* (South Bend: St. Augustine's Press).

Koslowski, P. (1988), *Prinzipien der ethischen Ökonomie* (Tübingen: Mohr).

Layard, R. (2005), *Happiness, Lessons from a New Science* (London: Allen Lane).

Lenoir, F. (2009), *Socrate, Jésus, Bouddha: Trois maîtres de vie* (Fayard).

Leonard, A. (2014), *Sharing economy* shams: deception at the core of the Internet's hottest businesses. How companies like Airbnb use the language of "sharing" and "gifts" to conceal ambitions far more libertarian, *Salon*, 14 March.

Levinas, E. (1986), *Socialité et Argent* (Antwerp: Belgische Spaarbankenvereniging).

Levinas, E. (2012), *Totality and Infinity* (Dordrecht: Kluwer Academic).

Libbrecht, U. (2014), *Adieu à Dieu* (Antwerp: Garrant).

Locke, J. (1689) *Two Treatises on Government.*

Macintyre, A. (1981), *After Virtue, A Study in Moral Theory* (London: Duckworth).

Manuel, F. (1979), *Utopian Thought in the Western World* (Oxford: Basil Blackwell).

Maris, B. (2014), *Houellebecq économiste* (Paris: Flammarion).

Maritain, J. (1936), *Humanisme intégral* (Paris: Aubier).

Mason, P. (2016), *Postcapitalism: A Guide to Our Future* (New York: Farrar, Straus & Giroux).

Meadows, D. (1972), *The Limits to Growth* (New York: Universe Books).

Mensink, W. (2015), *Kun je een betere wereld kopen?* (Amsterdam: Boom).

Milanovic, B. (2016), *Global Inequality. A New Approach for the Age of Globalization* (Cambridge: Harvard University Press).

Moesen, W. J. Schollaert (2002), *De kwaliteit van de overheid in Euroland* (Leuven: Mimeo).

More, T. (1737), *Utopia* (trans. Gilbert Burnet) (Dublin: Reilly).

More, T. (2010) *Utopia* (trans. G.C. Richards and W. P. Weaver) (Peterborough: Broadview Press).

More, T. (1912), *The Utopia of* (ed. William Armes) (New York: Macmillan).

Morus, T. (2014), *Utopia* (Amsterdam: Polak & Van Gennep).

Noels, G. (2008), *Econoshock* (Tielt: Lannoo).

Nussbaum, M. (2010), *Not for Profit, Why Democracy Needs the Humanities* (Princeton: Princeton University Press).

Nussbaum, M. and A. Sen (1993), *The Quality of Life* (New York/Oxford: Clarendon Press/Oxford University Press).

Nussbaum, M. (2001), *Upheavals of Thought, The Intelligence of Emotions* (Cambridge: Cambridge University Press).

Onfray, M. (2016), *Penser l'Islam* (Paris: Grasset).

Opdebeeck, H. (1986), *Schumacher Is Beautiful* (Kapellen: Pelckmans).

Opdebeeck, H., W. Thys and T. Vandevelde (1989), *Economie, macht en gerechtigheid* (Kapellen: Pelckmans).

Opdebeeck, H. (1992), Schumachers "intermediaire" economie. In L. Bouckaert, *Metafysiek en engagement: een personalistische visie op gemeenschap en economie* (Leuven: Acco), pp. 273–89.

Opdebeeck, H. (1995), *Bank, Stad en Kathedraal* (Kapellen: Pelckmans).

Opdebeeck, H., L. Anckaert and D. Cassimon (2002), *Building Towers: Perspectives on Globalization* (Leuven: Peeters).

Opdebeeck, H. (2007), Globalization between market and democracy. In F. Peat (ed.), *The Pari Dialogues. Essays in Science, Religion, Society and the Arts* (Grosseto: Pari), pp. 224–40.

Opdebeeck, H., L. Bouckaert and L. Zsolnai (2008), *Frugality: Rebalancing Material and Spiritual Values in Economic Life* (Oxford: Peter Lang).

Opdebeeck, H. (2010a), The collaborative enterprise as a linkage between principle and practice, in A.Tancati (ed.), *The collaborative enterprise: creating values for a sustainable world* (Bern: Peter Lang), pp. 39–62.

Opdebeeck, H. (2010b), Compassionate leadership as an expression of the common good, in H.-C. de Bettignies (ed.), Leadership, spirituality and the common good (Antwerp: Garant), pp. 115–28.

Opdebeeck, H. (2010c), Respect and democracy, the legacy of Jacques Maritain's Humanism Intégral, in L. Bouckaert, *Respect and Economic Democracy* (Antwerp: Garant), pp. 55–70.

Opdebeeck, H. and A. Habisch (2011a), Compassion: Chinese and Western perspectives on practical wisdom in management, *Journal of Management Development*, 3017/8, pp. 778–88.

Opdebeeck, H. (2011b), Planet and people-centered economics, in L. Bouckaert, *Handbook of spirituality and business* (New York: Palgrave Macmillan), pp. 171–8.

Opdebeeck, H. and L. Zsolnai (eds) (2011c), *Spiritual Humanism and Economic Wisdom* (Antwerp: Garant).

Opdebeeck, H. (2012), Responsibility in a globalised environment, in *Journal of Global Responsibility*, 3(1), pp. 111–20.

Opdebeeck, H. (ed.) (2013a), *Responsible Economics* (Bern: Peter Lang).

Opdebeeck, H. (2013b), The role of the charismatic economist E. F. Schumacher in economic and civil life: CSR and beyond, in L.Bruni (ed.) (2013), *The Charismatic Principle in Social Life* (Routledge: London), pp. 151–70.

Opdebeeck, H. (2015), The wisdom of mercy as the foundation of business and peace: the alternative to fear, in L. Bouckaert (ed.), *Business, Ethics and Peace* (Bingley: Emerald Group), pp. 63–74.

Opdebeeck, H. (2017), *Troost in Muziek* (Antwerp: Pelckmans).

Parret, H. (1989), *In alle redelijkheid, Standpunten over het denken, spreken en handelen van de redelijke mens* (Meppel: Boom).

Pauli, G. (2010), *The Blue Economy* (Taos: Paradigm Publications).

Pelckmans, P. (2015), Ivan Illich en het bederf van het beste, *Streven*, July–Aug., pp. 618–29.

Piketty, T. (2014), *Kapitaal in de 21ste eeuw* (Amsterdam: De Bezige Bij).

Provisional Findings of 2015 GNH Survey (2015) (Thimphu: Centre for Bhutan Studies & GNH, Research), ISBN 978-99936-14-80-8.

Ricoeur, P. (1964), *Histoire et Vérité* (Paris: Seuil).

Ricoeur, P. (1975), Le problème du fondement de la morale, *Sapienza*, 28(1), March, pp. 313–37.

Ricoeur, P. (1968), *Politiek en geloof* (Utrecht: Ambo).

Ricoeur, P. (1990), *Soi-même comme un autre* (Paris: Seuil).

Roose, K. (2014), The sharing economy isn't about trust, it's about desperation, *New York Magazine*, 24 Apr.

Ross, D. and H. Kincaid (2009), *The Oxford Handbook of Philosophy of Economics* (Oxford: Oxford University Press).

Roubini, N. and S. Mihm (2011), *Crisis Economics: A Crash Course in the Future of Finance* (London: Penguin).

Rousseau, J.-J. (1755), *Discours sur l'origine et les fondements de l'inégalité parmi les hommes* (Paris).

Sachs, J., L. Becchetti and A. Annett (2016), *World Happiness Report 2016, Special Rome Edition (Vol. II)* (New York: Sustainable Development Solutions Network).

Schumacher, E. F. (1973), *Small Is Beautiful* (London: Blond & Briggs).

Scruton, R. (2016), *The Soul of the World* (Princeton: Princeton University Press).

Sebregaondi, L. and T. Parks (2011), *Money and Beauty. Bankers, Botticelli and the Bonfire of the Vanities* (Florence: Giunti).

Sedlacek, T. (2011), *Economics of Good and Evil: The Quest for Economic Meaning from Gilgamesh to Wall Street* (Oxford: Oxford University Press).

Sen, A. (1987), *On Ethics and Economics* (Oxford: The Royer Lectures).

Shaughnessy, H. (2015), *Shift, A User's Guide to the New Economy* (London: The Disruption House).

Stiglitz, J. (2002), *Globalization and Its Discontents* (New York: Norton).

Stiglitz, J. (2015), *Rewriting the Rules of the American Economy: An Agenda for Growth and Shared Prosperity* (New York: Norton).

Taels, J. (1994), Ethiek en subjectiviteit, *Bijdragen*, 55, pp. 137–8.

Tawney, R. (1938), *Religion and the Rise of Capitalism. A Historical Study* (Harmondsworth: Pelican).

Thackara, J. (2015), *How to Thrive in the Next Economy* (London: Thames & Hudson).

Thomas à Kempis (2009), *De navolging van Christus* ('s-Hertogenbosch: KBS).

Tillich, P. (1952), *The Courage to Be* (New Haven: Yale University Press).

Tocqueville, A. de (1848), *De la démocratie en Amérique* (Paris: Pagnière).

Vandevelde, A. (ed.) (2000), *Over vertrouwen en bedrijf* (Leuven/Den Haag: Acco).

Van Oyen, G. (2008), *Albert Schweizer* (Budel: Damon).

Van Bladel, L. (1980), Geweld, religie en christendom, *Streven*, Oct., pp. 10–26.

Van Bladel, L. (1993), Authentieke economie en ethische hiërarchie, in K. Boey (ed.), *Een prijswaardige economie* (Brussels: Selektief-Infotex).

Vanheeswijck, G. (2016), *De draad van Penelope, Europa tussen ironie en waarheid* (Antwerp: Polis).

Van Isacker, K. (1970), Het land van de dwazen (Antwerp: Nederlandse Boekhandel).

Van Oyen, G. (2008), *Albert Schweitzer. Voor het leven* (Budel: Damon).

Van Parijs, P. (1991), *Qu'est-ce-qu'une société juste? Introduction à la pratique de la philosophie politique* (Paris: Seuil).

Van Parijs, P. (1997), *Real Freedom for All: What (If Anything) Can Justify Capitalism?* (Oxford: Oxford University Press).

Van Rompuy, P. (2016), *Economie zoekt Geluk, Hoe worden we welvarender en gelukkiger?* (Tielt: Lannoo).

Versteylen, L. (1981), *Wij hebben ze niet meer alle vijf* (Borgerhout: Uitgeverij Stil Leven).

Wijngaards, A. and E. Sent (2014), De wisselwerking tussen zingeving en economie, *M&O: Tijdschrift voor Management en Organisatie*, 5/6, pp. 62–73.

Wilkinson, N. (2008), *An Introduction to Behavioral Economics* (Basingstoke/New York: Palgrave Macmillan).

Zsolnai,L. (2018), *Ethics, Meaning and Market Society* (New York: Routledge).

Series Titles

The Economy and Meaningfulness. A Utopia, Hendrik Opdebeeck, n° 30, 2018, 136 p., ISBN 978-2-8076-0964-8

Forme(s) et modes d'être / Form(s) and Modes of Being. L'ontologie de Roman Ingarden / The Ontology of Roman Ingarden, Olivier Malherbe, Richard Sébastien, n° 29, 2016, 246 p., ISBN 978-2-87574-357-2

The Point of Philosophy. An Introduction for the Human Sciences, Ludo Abicht, Hendrik Opdebeeck, n° 28, 2015, 152 p., ISBN 978-2-87574-312-1

Redesigning Life. Eugenics, Biopolitics, and the Challenge of the Techno-Human Condition, Nathan Van Camp, No. 27, 2015, 166 p., ISBN 978-2-87574-281-0

Lotze et son héritage. Son influence et son impact sur la philosophie du XXe siècle, Federico boccaccini (dir.), No. 26, 2015, 274 p., ISBN 978-2-87574-278-0

Confiance réflexive et institutionnalisme. Des théories libérales du choix rationnel à la gouvernance du fait social monétaire, Benjamin Six, No. 25, 2013, 226 p., ISBN 978-2-87574-092-2

A Study in Transborder Ethics: Justice, Citizenship, Civility, Geneviève Souillac, No. 24, 2012, 221 p., ISBN 978-90-5201-824-9

Creative Crises of Democracy, Joris Gijsenber Gh, Saskia Hollander, Tim Houwen & Wim de Jong (eds.), No. 23, 2012, 444 p., ISBN 978-90-5201-797-6

Philosophical Essays. Critic Rationalism as Historical-objective Transcendentalism, Giulio Preti, edited by Fabio Minazzi, No. 22, 2011, 326 p., ISBN 978-90-5201-778-5

Regards éthiques sur l'Union européenne, Ignace Berten, Gabriel Fragnière, Philippe D. Grosjean, Peter Knauer, Daniel Spoel et Frank Turner, No. 21, 2011, 251 p., ISBN 978-90-5201-737-2

Responsibility and Cultures of the World. Dialogue around a Collective Challenge, Edith sizoo (ed.), No. 20, 2010, 243 p., ISBN 978-90-5201-670-2

Between Enlightenment and Disaster. Dimensions of the Political Use of Knowledge, Linda Sangolt (ed.), No. 19, 2010, 171 p., ISBN 978-90-5201-631-3

Variations sur la confiance. Concepts et enjeux au sein des théories de la gouvernance, Claire Lobet-Maris, Robin Lucas & Benjamin Six (dir.), No. 18, 2009, 206 p., ISBN 978-90-5201-525-5

La cosmodémocratie. Un principe de gouvernance pour la société technologique et mondialisée, René Ngambele Nsasay, No. 17, 2008, 310 p., ISBN 978-90-5201-463-0

Un droit, des morales. Valoriser l'État laïque, Paul LöwenthaL, No. 16, 2008, 156 p., ISBN 978-90-5201-442-5

Robert Schuman: Neo Scholastic Humanism and the Reunification of Europe, Alan Fimister, No. 15, 2008, 284 p., ISBN 978-90-5201-439-5

Science and Ethics. The Axiological Contexts of Science, Evandro Agazzi & Fabio Minazzi (eds.), No. 14, 2008, ISBN 978-90-5201-426-5

Rôles, action sociale et vie subjective. Recherches à partir de la phénoménologie de Michel Henry, Raphaël Gély, n° 13, 2007, 205 p., ISBN 978-90-5201-347-3

Identités et monde commun. Psychologie sociale, philosophie, société, Raphaël Gély, n° 12, 2006 (3e tirage 2008), 206 p., ISBN 978-90-5201-416-6

Feminists Contest Politics and Philosophy, Lisa N. Gurley, Claudia Leeb & Anna Aloisia Moser (eds.), No. 11, 2005, 272 p., ISBN 978-90-5201-252-0

The Importance of Ideals. Debating Their Relevance in Law, Morality, and Politics, Wibren Van der Burg & Sanne Taekema (eds.), No. 10, 2004, 274 p., ISBN 978-90-5201-226-1

Social Sciences and Political Change. Promoting Innovative Research in Post-Socialist Countries, Robin Cassling & Gabriel Fragnière (eds.), No. 9, 2003, 297 p., ISBN 978-90-5201-168-4

Working-Class Women in Elite Academia. A Philosophical Inquiry, Claudia Leeb, No. 8, 2004, 220 p., ISBN 978-90-5201-979-6

L'autonomie éthique. Débat démocratique et vérité, Giuseppe G. Nastri, n° 7, 2002, 200 p., ISBN 978-90-5201-972-7

Plus est en l'homme. Le personnalisme vécu comme humanisme radical, Vincent Triest, n° 6, 2000 (4e tirage 2004), 214 p., ISBN 978-90-5201-922-2

Enlightenment and Genocide, Contradictions of Modernity, James Kaye & Bo Stråth (eds.), No. 5, 2000, 278 p., ISBN 978-90-5201-919-2

Les défis du nationalisme moderne. Québec, Catalogne, Écosse, Michael Keating, n° 4, 1997, 298 p., ISBN 978-90-5201-705-1

www.peterlang.com